William Tecumseh Sherman

Defender of the Union

by Wyatt Blassingame
illustrated by Ron Lesser
general editor, Arthur Orrmont

 A Rutledge Book

Prentice-Hall, Inc.
Englewood Cliffs, New Jersey

SBN 13-959742-5
Copyright © 1970 by Rutledge Books, Inc.
All rights reserved
Prepared and produced by Rutledge Books, Inc.
Published by Prentice-Hall, Inc.
Englewood Cliffs, New Jersey
Library of Congress Catalog Card Number 69–10332
Printed in the United States of America

Contents

HALL OF FAME BOOKS

All of the books in this series of biographies are recreations of the lives of famous Americans—specifically those Americans who have been elected to the Hall of Fame of New York University. Outstanding men and women of many fields are honored here: authors, educators, preachers and theologians, humanitarians, social and economic reformers, scientists, engineers, architects, physicians and surgeons, inventors, missionaries and explorers, military leaders, lawyers and judges, statesmen, businessmen, philanthropists, artists. The Hall of Fame is located on the campus of New York University on high ground commanding views of the Harlem and Hudson River valleys. There, in an open colonnade, are displayed the bronze busts of those honored. It is a national educational and patriotic shrine belonging to the people of this country. There are niches for one hundred busts, of which ninety-three have been filled.

Other Hall of Fame Books:

John Adams: Reluctant Patriot of the Revolution
James Monroe: Hero of American Diplomacy
Joseph Henry: Father of American Electronics
James B. Eads: The Man Who Mastered
  the Mississippi   .
Alice Freeman Palmer: Pioneer College President

William
Tecumseh
Sherman

1

A New Home and a New Name

The boy was nine years old, with bright-red, unruly hair. His eyes were big; against his thin face they sometimes looked dark blue, sometimes black, sometimes brown. Even his father and mother argued about the color of his eyes. But whatever their color, they were always bright and alert. Sitting at his school desk, Tecumseh Sherman was supposed to be studying, but now he glanced up at the little girl who had entered the classroom and was whispering to the teacher.

The teacher's face became suddenly very serious. "Tecumseh," he said.

"Yes, sir?"

"You and your sisters, Amelia and Julia Ann, are wanted at home." Tecumseh's sisters, sitting a few rows away, were both slightly older than he. The school in the little town of Lancaster, Ohio, had only two teachers, so several classes had to be held in each room of the two-room schoolhouse.

"Home?" Tecumseh asked. He had never been

called away from school in the middle of the day. "All of us?"

"All of you." The teacher's voice was solemn. "Your brothers Lampson and John, from the other classroom, are waiting for you. You may leave your books here."

"Yes, sir."

Slowly the Sherman children left the classroom. In the hall they met Lampson, eight, and John, six. "Why are we going home at this time of day?" John asked.

No one answered him because no one knew the reason. The children walked quietly along the unpaved street. It was early June 1829; the sun was bright and the trees were green with new leaves. A horse and buggy passed and the driver looked curiously at the children. "What are you youngsters doing out of school?" he called, but didn't wait for an answer.

John pulled at Tecumseh's jacket. "Cump?"

Practically everyone called him "Cump." His father had named him Tecumseh, for the famous Indian chief, but his brothers and sisters hadn't been able to pronounce the name. "Cump," John asked now, "is something wrong?"

"I don't know." Still, he had a feeling. He was sure that something had gone wrong at home, though he had no idea what it might be.

When they reached home, the children's grandmother was waiting for them, surrounded by the three youngest Sherman children. Elizabeth, their 17-year-old sister, was there, too. She had been crying.

"Your father is very sick," the grandmother

told them. "He's in a town called Lebanon, about a hundred miles away. Your mother is packing now to go to him."

The children looked at one another. Their father, Charles Sherman, was a judge who had to travel a great deal, going from town to town to hold court. He had been perfectly well when he left home only a few days before.

Their mother came down the stairs. A carriage was waiting out front and she barely had time to kiss the children good-bye. Then the carriage rolled away, powdery dust rising around its wheels.

A few hours later it was back again. Mrs. Sherman was weeping. A neighbor helped her into the house. The children watched, large-eyed and frightened. Cump could never remember just how he learned what had happened.

Mrs. Sherman's carriage had gone only a few miles when it was met by a man who told her there was no need to go ahead. Judge Sherman had died in Lebanon. No one knew why, not even the doctor.

Judge Sherman had been a well-educated, highly respected man. Before being judge he had been tax collector. When two of his assistants made an error of several thousand dollars, Charles Sherman had taken it on himself to pay off the debt, even though he was not responsible for it. The debt had been paid, but it left Judge Sherman practically penniless. After his death, his wife learned she had an income of only $400 a year. And eleven children! Even with the two oldest boys away at work, there were nine children to feed and clothe.

Cump was too young to understand the problem fully. Even so, he was the oldest boy left at home. He and Lampson, with John tagging after them, spent hours trying to figure what they could do to help their mother. There was, however, very little that eight- and nine-year-old boys could do.

A few weeks after Judge Sherman's death, Cump and his younger brothers were playing in the yard when Mr. Thomas Ewing came past. Mr. Ewing was a successful lawyer who lived only a few doors up the street from the Shermans. He and Judge Sherman had been close friends and Mr. Ewing's oldest son Philemon was the same age as Cump. Now Mr. Ewing stopped and stared for a long moment at the boys in the yard. Then he went into the Sherman house.

Minutes later he was back, this time with Mrs. Sherman and Elizabeth. Together they stood looking at the three boys. Their faces were so solemn it made Cump nervous. He quit playing and watched them.

"Which one shall I take?" Mr. Ewing said.

Mrs. Sherman held one hand against her mouth. She was trying to keep from crying. Cump moved quickly to stand beside her. After a moment she told him, "Mr. Ewing has offered to—take one of you. To raise. It—it will help me. But—" Her voice broke.

Suddenly 17-year-old Elizabeth bent forward, put her arm around Cump and turned him toward Mr. Ewing. "Take Cump," she said. "He's the smartest."

Cump felt a sudden flash of terror. He knew

10

the Ewing home well. He liked both Mr. and Mrs. Ewing and had often spent the night with Philemon. But there was a big difference between going away from his own home for one night and going away to live.

Mrs. Sherman knelt in front of Cump. There were tears in her eyes. "You can walk down the hill to see us every day," she said. And then, "You'll be happy with the Ewings?" It was half statement, half question.

Cump couldn't answer because of the lump in his throat, but he managed to nod.

From that day both Mr. and Mrs. Ewing treated Cump as if he were their own son. He and Phil played and fought together like brothers, largely ignoring Ellen Ewing who was only four years old, and Hugh Ewing who was three.

It was a pleasant life for a boy. Lancaster was a small town in what was then thought of as the West. There were woods and ponds nearby where the children played.

The greatest danger in the woods—or so Cump and his friends believed—was the fabled hoop snake. The hoop snake was supposed to be able to put its tail in its own mouth, form a hoop and roll so fast no boy could outrun it. When the snake caught up with its victim, it would stab him in the seat of the pants with a poisonous pair of horns that grew on its head.

Cump always carried a large stick in the woods with which to fight the hoop snake. He also invented his first military plan to outwit it. If a hoop snake ever got after him, Cump said, he would run toward a large tree. Then, just as the snake went to stab him with its horns, he would jump to one side. The snake would stick its horns in the tree and be caught fast and Cump could kill it easily with his club.

Quite naturally, neither Cump nor any of his friends ever encountered a hoop snake. By the time he was 13, he had quit believing in such things. But now he had a new problem. His foster-father had given him a gun. Cump liked to hunt and preferred going alone, moving quietly through the woods to stalk the rabbits and squirrels he shot. But little Hugh and Ellen Ewing often wanted to tag along. When Cump refused, they would follow him anyway, calling, "Redheaded woodpecker! You're a redheaded woodpecker!"

It seemed to Cump that everybody teased him about his red hair. Cump never cared much about the way he looked—except for that red hair. It stuck out from his head in six different directions, but even that wouldn't have mattered so much if it hadn't been for the color. In desperation he decided to do something about it.

When no one was looking, Cump took some of the dye that Mrs. Ewing used in her housework. He wanted to make his hair a sort of light brown that nobody would notice. None of the dyes seemed exactly the right color, so he mixed two or three of them together, added water and washed his hair. Then he went and looked in the mirror.

His hair was now a bright green. Frantically he washed it in clear water—and it was still green. He washed it again, and it stayed green.

Eventually he gave up. For the next few weeks he wore his cap indoors and outdoors, pulled down hard on his head. Some people teased him until he was ready to fight or cry or both. When finally his hair grew out red again, it was so much better than being green that he quit worrying about it.

Cump's former home wasn't far away. He enjoyed visiting his family, but in the course of time he had become a member of the Ewing family.

Since Mr. Ewing was a successful lawyer, many prominent people came to visit him. Among them were senators and congressmen. When Cump had been two years with the Ewings, Mr. Ewing was appointed United States senator by the Ohio legislature. Now much of his time had to be spent in Washington, but when he was home, more and more famous people came to call. Naturally Cump heard a great deal of talk about politics and most of it bored him. But there was one point about which Senator Ewing felt so strongly that Cump, who greatly admired his foster-father, couldn't help but listen with interest.

Congress had passed a law with which many people in South Carolina did not agree. Some of these people were saying that if a state didn't like a federal law, then the state need not obey it. There was talk of South Carolina withdrawing from the Union.

With all his heart Senator Thomas Ewing believed in the Union. When President Andrew Jackson said he would force South Carolina to remain in the Union even if it meant war, Senator Ewing

13

cheered. He did not belong to the same party as the President, but to Ewing the Union was far more important than any party. In Congress, Daniel Webster made a speech that ended, "Liberty and union, now and forever, one and inseparable!" Senator Ewing read this speech to his family and quoted it over and over.

To young Cump Sherman the idea of the Union became almost a religion, just as it was to his foster-father.

Religion, to Cump's foster-mother, was a much simpler matter. She was a devout Catholic. From the first it worried her that Cump had never been baptized. Eventually she walked down the hill to talk with Mrs. Sherman. A priest was coming to visit, she said. Would it be all right to have Cump baptized?

Mrs. Sherman said yes.

When the priest arrived on horseback, the Ewing family gathered in the parlor—there was no Catholic church in Lancaster—for the ceremony. "What is your name?" the priest asked Cump.

"Tecumseh."

For a moment the priest looked startled. Then he smiled. "That's an Indian name. For baptism you must have a Christian name. Is there any you prefer?"

Cump shook his head.

"Today is the Feast of St. William," the priest said. "I will baptize you William Tecumseh."

So it was that Tecumseh Sherman acquired a new name. It didn't really matter. Everybody kept right on calling him Cump.

2

West Point

As a United States senator, Thomas Ewing had the right to appoint boys to the Military Academy at West Point. No boy could attend the Academy until he was at least 16 years old, but Senator Ewing planned ahead. Cump had been born on February 8, 1820; he wouldn't be 16 until 1836. Even so, in 1833 Senator Ewing wrote from Washington to his wife in Lancaster, "Tell Cumpy that I want him to learn fast that he may be ready to go to West Point. . . ."

The Academy meant very little to Cump at the time. All he knew about West Point was that it was very strict and that after graduation he would go into the army. He had never thought much about the army one way or another, and he still didn't. He was a quiet, steady boy. His grades in school were good. He wanted to continue his education, and if his foster-father wanted him to go to West Point, he was glad to go.

In May 1836 Cump left for West Point. He

15

was to go first to Washington to visit Senator Ewing, then on to the Academy.

At 16, Cump had never been more than a few miles from home, and never on his own. He was a little afraid, but he hid his fear. He climbed into the stagecoach, waved good-bye to his mother and foster-mother, to all the little Ewings and Shermans gathered around them. The driver's whip cracked. The coach rolled down the dusty street, past the houses Cump knew so well—and on into the country toward a new life.

This was the great National Road, the nation's chief east-west thoroughfare. Even so, it wasn't much of a highway. The four horses that pulled the coach had to be changed every ten miles. When the road was muddy, as it was after every rain, the coach would often bog down. Then the passengers had to get out and push while the driver whipped and shouted at his horses.

Nine passengers could ride inside the coach while another rode on top with the driver. Cump liked to ride on top whenever he could; from there he could see better. His eyes that seemed almost to change color with his thoughts studied the countryside, the springtime green of the trees, the wild flowers on the hillsides, the strange towns. All his life he had a remarkable ability to remember landscapes, the location of hills and streams and houses. It was almost as if his eyes photographed the things he saw and stored the pictures away in his head, to be recalled in detail whenever he wished.

Traveling day and night, it took three days to go from Lancaster, Ohio, to Frederick, Maryland,

a distance of little more than three hundred miles.
In Frederick, Cump had to make a decision. From
here he could take a smaller stagecoach, or he
could take a train. He had never been on a train
—had never even seen one. The idea of riding on
one both fascinated and frightened him. Telling
about it later he would say he didn't have "full
faith" in the train. So he took a two-horse stagecoach on to Washington. There he found Senator
Ewing, as Cump wrote to his family back in Lancaster, "boarding with a mess of Senators at Mrs.
Hill's and I transferred my trunk to the same place."

The one thing Cump remembered best about
his visit to Washington was an hour spent standing just outside the White House fence watching
President Andrew Jackson. The tall, stiffly erect
old gentleman paced back and forth across the
White House lawn. His hair was white, but Cump
knew it had once been as red as his own. He wondered if anybody had ever teased Andrew Jackson
about having red hair.

Cump spent a week in Washington. From
there he took his first train ride to New York City,
then continued on to West Point.

Cump had never seen anything quite like West
Point. Fifty miles above New York City the great
Hudson River cut through wild, heavily wooded
hills, dark green in early summer. Sixteen-year-old
Cump could imagine bear, deer, even Indians
maybe, prowling silently among the trees.

The school itself, however, disappointed and
depressed him. All his life he would be given to
moods, on top of the world one day, deep in gloom

17

the next, and his early days at West Point were gloomy ones indeed. The Academy was built around a large, open, tree-rimmed plain. The buildings were of gray stone, two to four stories high, looking stiff, cold and ugly.

The new boys, called plebes, were put in crowded barracks. Cump shared with two other boys a small room whose furniture consisted of three mattresses and three straight-back chairs. There was nothing else, except a fireplace for heat. In a letter to Senator Ewing, Cump apologized for his handwriting—he had to use his chair for a desk while sitting on the floor.

First there were the entrance examinations to be passed. Cump had no trouble with them; he had studied hard back in Lancaster and the exams were easy. At this time Congress wanted West Point to be available to almost any boy, whether or not he had had the advantage of a good education. The first year studies consisted mostly of math and French. The French was necessary because many of the military textbooks to be studied were written in that language.

Although Cump had no trouble with his studies, he found the discipline very strict, accustomed as he was to the easygoing life of the Ewing household. At West Point a bugle blew at first daylight and Cump had to jump up from his mattress, dress hurriedly in a uniform with a high, stiff collar, a short gray coat and tight trousers. Next the room had to be cleaned, the bed perfectly made. After that the plebes were supposed to sit in their chairs, breakfastless, and study till seven o'clock.

At seven, another bugle blew and the students marched to breakfast. They ate sitting stiffly at long tables. Afterward they marched off to classes.

Dinner was at one o'clock. After that there were more classes until four. Then came drill on the big parade ground in front of the buildings. This was the part that Cump liked best, except sometimes in the winter when a bitter wind swept down the Hudson and his ears felt as though they had turned to ice and were about to fall off.

Drill ended at six o'clock. The cadets stood at attention while the bugle played and the flag came down. Supper followed, after which the cadets went back to their quarters where they were supposed to study until ten o'clock. Then came lights out.

If Cump liked the drill best, he liked the frequent inspections least. He and his roommates had to stand stiffly at attention while the inspecting officer moved around the room. Cump had always been careless about the way he dressed, and now he was constantly getting demerits.

Students were rated both by grades and conduct. One demerit was given for such things as unshined shoes or a spot of rust on a belt buckle. Missing drill cost eight demerits. Fortunately Cump missed few drills: he got enough demerits in other ways. Many years later a general who had been a cadet at West Point with him wrote, "Cump usually had a grease spot on his pants from clandestine night feasts. . . . We stole boiled potatoes in handkerchiefs and stuffed them under our vests; we poked butter into our gloves. . . . We stole bread, and when we got together at night 'Old Cump'

19

would mix everything into a hash and cook it in a stew pan over the fire. He was the best hash maker at West Point."

If a cadet got two hundred demerits in one year, he could be dismissed no matter how good his grades. At the end of his first year Cump had 109 black marks against his name. This made him 124th in conduct out of the entire student body of 211. On the other hand, of the 76 cadets in his class, only eight had better grades.

There was no vacation at the end of Cump's first year. Instead, the class moved out of the barracks to camp in tents on the big plain in front of the school. Now the days were spent in drill, in learning to handle guns and swords and horses.

With fall the cadets moved back into barracks and longer hours of study. There were no sports at West Point, no organized recreation. With almost nothing to do besides study, drill and steal food, Cump spent long hours writing letters to his family. Often he wrote to his little foster-sister Ellen, who was 12 now. Ellen kept all his letters and carefully answered each one.

By now Cump was learning how to keep his clothes neat and his shoes shined. His second year he got only 48 demerits. In his studies he stood very near the top of his class, with only five cadets ahead of him.

At West Point many of the cadets were from the South, and naturally there was a great deal of talk about slavery. Sitting in front of an open fire in Cump's room one night a handsome, olive-skinned boy from Louisiana, Pierre Gustave Toutant

Beauregard, explained how most people in the South felt.

"When the Abolitionists in the North talk about freeing the slaves," he said, "they really mean they want to destroy the South. Slaves are property worth thousands of dollars. To take the slaves away from their masters would be the same as going into a Northern state and taking a man's home and business away from him."

"But what if the government paid the slave owners to give up their slaves?" asked a cadet from Vermont.

"Most Abolitionists don't want to pay," replied Beauregard. "Even if they did, it wouldn't help much. The economy of the South depends on raising cotton and sugar cane. Only Negroes can do that work. And they won't work if they're free. Paying to free slaves would be like paying a man to burn his factory, then telling him he couldn't build another one. Once his money was spent he'd have nothing, and no way to earn a living."

Cump listened but said nothing. He knew very little about slavery, and it didn't bother him one way or the other. In fact, most of the West Point cadets, including many from the North, agreed with the Southern point of view on slavery.

Yet there were some, even some from the South, who had doubts. One of these was Cump's best friend, a fat, serious-faced boy named George Thomas. "Old Tom" the cadets called him, because he looked older than he was. Thomas came from Virginia; his family owned slaves, and like most of the Southerners he agreed that slavery was eco-

GENERAL GEORGE H. THOMAS

nomically necessary. And yet at the same time there were things about it he couldn't stomach. "You know," he told Cump, "in many Southern states it's against the law to teach a Negro how to read or write, to give him any education."

"I've heard that," Cump said.

The fat boy rubbed his chin thoughtfully. "I can't believe that's right," he said. "At home we laugh at slaves for being superstitious and believing in silly things. But how can they know better, if we force them to stay ignorant?"

Cump didn't answer, and Thomas said, "When I was a little boy, just learning to read, I used to meet with some of the Negro children every day after I got out of school. We'd hide in the bushes and I'd teach them what I'd learned that day. I don't know what my family would have said, if they'd known about it. But I thought I was right."

It was a conversation that meant little to Cump at the time, but many years later he would remember it in detail. When the Civil War began

George Thomas fought with the Union. President Lincoln, who knew Thomas' home had been in Virginia, wondered about his loyalty. There was no need to wonder, Sherman told Lincoln: George Thomas was a man who would do what he thought was right and keep doing it, no matter what.

After his second year at West Point, Cump Sherman was given a summer vacation. He went home to Lancaster, where little Ellen Ewing followed him around like a puppy, very proud of him in his uniform.

In the fall he returned to the Point. His studies were more interesting now, his demerits fewer, his letters to Ellen longer and more frequent. But there was no vacation after his third year and he didn't get home again.

During Cump's last year at the Academy a short, shy, awkward plebe arrived whose name was registered as U.S. Grant. Grant kept saying, a little bashfully, that there really wasn't any "S" in his name. It had been mistakenly added by the congressman who appointed him to West Point. But the name stuck, though Cump, who had sometimes been teased about his own name, took no part in calling the little plebe "Uncle Sam" or "United States" Grant. In fact, separated by three years in their ages, they knew one another only slightly.

Cump never really enjoyed his life at the Academy and never held any student rank of importance. But he graduated along with his class and as a second lieutenant of artillery was assigned to duty in Florida, where the United States and the Seminole Indians were at war.

3

The Seminole War

In the fall of 1840, when Second Lieutenant Sherman arrived in Florida, the Seminole War had already been in progress for five years. For both the Indian and the white man it was a strange and frustrating conflict.

The Seminoles were not a single, closely knit tribe. The word "Seminole" meant Wild Ones, or Runaways, and was applied to all those Indians who had been driven out of Georgia and Alabama by encroaching white settlers and who had taken refuge in Florida. Now that the United States had acquired Florida from Spain, white settlers wanted this land also, and the federal government was determined to move the Seminoles to what was then considered worthless land in Oklahoma. The Seminoles were equally determined to keep their land in Florida.

They lacked the warriors to fight federal troops in pitched battles, and instead hit and ran. They burned the homes of settlers; they ambushed small parties of soldiers, firing a few shots, then disappearing into the surrounding swamp or forest. The troops in turn hunted the Indians as they might have hunted animals. They killed a few. They captured a few and sent them to Oklahoma. They burned the Indian villages and destroyed the fields of corn and pumpkins. They built forts all about southern Florida, designed to limit the Indians' freedom of movement.

It was to one of these bastions, called Fort Pierce, that Lieutenant Sherman was sent. Fighting had stopped in the area. In fact all the Indians seemed to have vanished, so the twenty-year-old officer had no chance to hear a gun fired in anger. But it was wonderful country for a young man who liked to hunt and fish.

In front of the fort was the Indian River. This was actually a long, narrow lagoon rather than a fresh-water river. It swarmed with redfish, trout and mackerel. These in turn were food for sharks, and Sherman learned to paddle a canoe and to spear sharks without upsetting the canoe. To the east, a string of low islands separated the Indian River from the open Atlantic. Here the swimming was good, and on summer nights huge green turtles crawled out of the sea onto the beach to lay their eggs. Cump Sherman learned to catch the turtles in the water with nets and, on the beach, roll them on their backs so they couldn't escape.

Sometimes he led small patrols inland, riding through cypress swamps where tall, moss-hung trees rose above the coffee-colored water. There was always the chance of ambush, the sudden crack of

25

gunfire and the whistle of arrows. But these things never happened. Cump had only one minor adventure with the Indians.

One day, without warning, several Seminoles appeared outside Fort Pierce with a white flag. Brought into the fort, they told the commanding officer that Cooacoochee, a chief the white men called Wild Cat, was nearby and wanted to talk about surrender. The commanding officer ordered Lieutenant Sherman to take a small group of soldiers and bring Wild Cat into the fort.

The Indians led Cump and his troopers along several miles of winding paths. Eventually the lieutenant began to get nervous. "How much farther?" he asked.

"Very near," he was told.

They went on. Finally, across the open prairie, Sherman saw Indians waiting for them by a thick clump of trees. Because of the trees, he couldn't be sure how many Seminoles were there. As his party drew close he turned to his soldiers. "Wait here. Don't raise your rifles, but be ready to use them if necessary." Then he rode on alone.

Cooacoochee came forward to meet him. He was young, strongly built, with high cheekbones and black hair. He wanted to hold the conference right there, in the open. "I have no authority to bargain with you," Sherman told him. "You must come to the fort, to my commanding officer—my chief."

Still the Indian hesitated. But as they talked Sherman noticed that all the Indians had leaned their rifles against the trees. Now the Indians were so intent on listening to their chief and to the white officer that they had forgotten the soldiers. Quietly Sherman motioned to his troopers. They moved forward and captured the Indians' guns by simply picking them up.

When Wild Cat noticed what had happened,

he merely shrugged. "I will go with you," he told Sherman, "but I must dress first."

Sherman knew of the Indian custom of putting on special clothes to hold a conference. He watched with great interest while Wild Cat pulled on several vests, obviously stolen from white settlers. One of these had a blood-stained bullet hole in it. Over the vest Wild Cat put on a coat, then a turban with ostrich plumes. "Now," he said and accompanied the lieutenant back to the fort. There Wild Cat made a bargain with the commanding officer to bring his followers but, as usual, nothing came of it.

Sherman missed the one small battle in which his company took part. Later he was both sorry and a little happy that he had been away at the time. He wrote Ellen Ewing that the fight had amounted to wounding two Indian females, one of them a child. He added, "You doubtless little sympathize with me in hunting and harassing a poor set of people who have had the heroism to defend their homes against such odds. . . ."

His sympathy now lay with the Indians. This wasn't the kind of war he had dreamed of fighting. But already he was learning that war is rarely a noble adventure and instead consists largely of suffering and evil. Yet it was the job of a soldier. And Cump Sherman was a soldier who would do his job.

When he had been in Florida for a year and a half, Sherman was promoted to first lieutenant and given a command of his own. This was a wilderness fort at Picalata on the bank of the St. Johns

River. There were no Indians in the area to cause trouble. The hunting was even better than at Fort Pierce. There were deer and wild turkey and bear and bobcat, and the river was filled with alligators and large bass.

As commanding officer he had a house of his own, a shack of palmetto logs with a thatched roof. The 21-year-old soldier turned it into a kind of zoo. Cump wrote Ellen that he had a pony that wandered in and out whenever it wished. A hen had her nest in one corner of his bedroom. In another corner he had made a bed for a pet fawn. He fed crows and cranes and other birds until they became so tame they would fly in and out of his house. Altogether it was one of the happiest times of his life.

After only a few months at Picalata, Lieutenant Sherman was transferred to Charleston, South Carolina. This was a post that most young officers considered the best in the country. There was very little work to do, and Charleston was the center of Southern social life. Young army officers were welcome in all the better homes. Sherman went to dances and parties by the dozens and made friends with many Southern families. And he began to paint pictures. He had had no formal lessons but had always been good at sketching landscapes.

In the summer of 1843 Cump returned to Lancaster, Ohio, on leave. He was 23 now, lean, quick-moving, his bright-red hair as unruly as ever. Ellen Ewing was 18, no longer a little girl but a young woman. Cump had always thought of her as his little sister, but of course she wasn't related to him at all. Before his leave was over, he and Ellen were engaged.

Perhaps they would have been married at this time, but as a first lieutenant Cump's salary was only $70 a month, and some of this he had to send to his mother. Ellen, accustomed to a big house and pretty clothes, would have been willing to accept money from her father. As a boy, Cump had lived in Senator Ewing's home at the senator's expense. "But it's different now," he told her. "I'm grown and have to earn my own way. I can't take money from your father any more."

"But he looks on you as one of his own sons," Ellen protested.

"I know. But I have to be independent now, if I'm to keep my self-respect."

So it was decided that marriage would have to wait until Cump was promoted to captain. When his leave was over he went back to South Carolina alone.

In the next few years Cump's postings carried him over much of South Carolina and Georgia. He was young and good-natured, he liked the Southern people and made friends easily. Riding horseback from town to town, he became thoroughly familiar with the hills and valleys and streams. Years later the knowledge that he stored away was to affect the fate of his Southern friends—and that of the nation itself.

Sherman had been in the South a little over four years when James K. Polk was elected President. One of the big issues of the campaign had been whether or not to take Texas into the Union.

Texas had once belonged to Mexico and Mexico still claimed it. Many people believed that the admission of Texas to the Union would mean war with Mexico. But most people, Polk along with them, wanted Texas. And in 1845 Texas was admitted to the Union as the 28th state.

Mexico did not go to war. And still President Polk was dissatisfied. Even more than Texas, he wanted California, which was also a part of Mexico. Polk tried to buy it, but the Mexicans refused.

Polk was determined to have California, even if it meant war with Mexico. But he was embarrassed to say so openly and had to find an excuse.

Up until that time most people had considered the Nueces River the southern border of Texas, but now Polk claimed that the Rio Grande was the southern border. He ordered troops across the Nueces. This finally forced Mexico into declaring war and gave Polk an excuse to invade California.

From the first Cump Sherman had hoped to be among the soldiers sent to Texas. If there was going to be a war, he wanted to be in it. Instead he was sent to Pittsburgh as a recruiting officer. This was his job when the fighting began.

"That I should be on recruiting service, when my comrades were actually fighting, was intolerable," Sherman wrote. Immediately he applied for a transfer. He wanted to go to Texas, to California, to anywhere there was fighting.

In a short time his orders came through. He was to report to New York. There he would join Company F of the Third Artillery and take a ship around Cape Horn to California.

4

California and the Gold Rush

In New York Lieutenant Sherman bought all the books about California he could find. There weren't many. Very little was known about that lush, far-off land.

Taking his books with him, Sherman boarded the *Lexington*, an ancient vessel converted from a sloop of war into a supply ship. On July 14, 1846, the ship raised its sails and turned slowly southward. In the long days that followed, the officers of Company F drilled their men on the deck for hours, simply to give them something to do. Sherman read his books on California and then read them again.

It took the *Lexington* two months to reach Rio de Janeiro, where it stopped to take on new supplies. Then the ship continued its southward voyage. Soon they were below the Tropic of Capricorn and the weather grew colder. By October, sailing close to shore, they could see the tops of snow-covered mountains. Off Cape Horn they ran into storms. For almost a full month the old sailing ship beat back and forth, trying to round the Horn and turn north. Part of the time it sailed close alongside a French sloop of war. Cump Sherman, bundled in his overcoat, stood for hours watching the other ship rise and fall with the tremendous waves.

Eventually the *Lexington* rounded Cape Horn. The weather improved. They crossed the Tropic of Capricorn, the Equator, the Tropic of Cancer. And on January 26, 1847, the *Lexington* dropped anchor off Monterey, California—198 days after leaving New York.

Lieutenant Sherman went ashore expecting to take part in the war against Mexico. But once again he was too late. Two months before, General Stephen Kearny had reached California by marching overland. His little army had fought several small but very bitter battles. In some parts of old Mexico the war was still going on, but in California the fighting was over. Once more Lieutenant William Sherman had gone through a war without firing a gun.

Back east it had seemed intolerable to Cump Sherman that his fellow officers should be fighting a war when he was not. Now it seemed even worse. He wrote to Ellen, "I have felt tempted to send my resignation to Washington, and I feel ashamed to wear epaulettes after having passed through a war without smelling gunpowder. . . ."

Then he learned that some of his West Point classmates had been promoted to captain. He had not, and bitterly he tried to resign. He wrote his

33

commanding officer, "Self-respect compels me therefore to quit the profession which in time of war and trouble I have failed to merit. . . ."

The resignation, however, never got beyond the commanding officer. "I'll hold it for awhile," he told the frustrated lieutenant. "Let's see if your mood doesn't change."

And Cump Sherman's mood did change. Except for his periods of depression, life in California wasn't bad. The country was beautiful, the weather good. He and his fellow officers often rode inland to hunt deer and bear. Each fall great flights of ducks and geese passed over the area. Sherman was commissary officer, and he sometimes killed enough ducks in a day to feed the entire company.

Once he was sent from Monterey to the little village of Yerba Buena. The village was actually nothing more than a few ramshackle shacks that seemed on the verge of being blown away by the wind that howled in off the bay. The single street was deep in drifting sand. Where the street reached the bay there was a small wharf; but when the tide was out, the wharf ended in mud, and even at high tide only small boats could reach it.

Another officer tried to persuade Lieutenant Sherman to buy land in Yerba Buena at 16 dollars for a large lot. "There's really an excellent harbor —once we get a decent wharf," he told Sherman. "And now that California belongs to the United States, the country is going to develop. I think the land here is a good investment."

Sherman laughed. "I wouldn't have the whole town if they gave it to me."

Later he wrote, "I felt actually insulted that he should think me such a fool as to pay money for property in such a horrid place as Yerba Buena. . . ." By that time, however, he was laughing at himself. Because Yerba Buena had grown —and had changed its name to San Francisco.

Sherman had been in California for a year and a half when he was called into the headquarters of Colonel R. B. Mason. Two other men in the room, dressed in rough, dirty clothes, stood at the colonel's desk. Colonel Mason pointed to some small rocks lying on his blotter. "Do you know what these are, Lieutenant?"

Sherman picked up the rocks and rolled them in his fingers. "Gold?" he asked.

"Have you ever seen gold?"

"Yes, sir. Several years ago when I was in Georgia. It didn't look exactly like this, but—" He put one of the rocks in his mouth and bit gently on it. It wasn't soft, but neither was it hard as an average rock.

"I think I can tell if it's gold," Sherman said. He went to the door and called for an enlisted man to bring him a hammer. Then, holding the rock with his left hand, he began to hit it with the hammer. The rock flattened out, but didn't break.

"It's gold, sir," Sherman said. "Where did it come from?"

Mason pointed to the two men. "They brought it. A man named John Sutter is building a sawmill up on American Fork and it was found there. Now Sutter wants to be sure he has title to the land."

Neither Sherman nor Colonel Mason had any

way of knowing how much gold would be found, and at first they paid little attention to the discovery. But soon a great many other persons were wildly excited. From Monterey and Yerba Buena and other settlements along the coast people began to rush inland to prospect for gold. Men who had driven wagon trains across the continent, intending to settle in Oregon, now poured into California.

The news spread eastward. From all across America men began to race toward the gold mines, by land and by sea, and the great California Gold Rush of 1849 was on. When they arrived, there was no housing for them, and little food. Prices of available goods went up and up. And the men kept coming.

At this time an army private made eight dollars a month. But any civilian working on the docks, the sawmills, the new frame houses that grew like mushrooms, could make 16 dollars a day. If he went inland to prospect for gold, he might make nothing, or he might reap a fortune. Newly arrived sailors deserted their ships, leaving them empty in San Francisco Bay. At Monterey and other army posts soldiers also began to desert.

One night Sherman was in his quarters talking with other officers when word came that 28 men had deserted that night. Everyone knew they were headed for the gold mines. "I can't really blame them," one officer said, "considering the money they'll make."

"But if they aren't forced to come back," Sherman said, "all the other soldiers will desert. We'll be left with an army post, and no army."

"It wouldn't do any good to send other soldiers after them. The ones we sent would just keep going."

"Then officers ought to go and bring them back."

"Could we find them?"

"We could find them," Sherman said confidently. He knew the country because he had hunted across it. "They've got to get across Salinas Plain, and the country there's so flat a rabbit can't cross it without being seen."

It was after midnight when seven officers, Sherman in the lead, left Monterey. The moon hung low in the west. Its misty light made the sandy road barely visible. Then the moon went down and in the dense darkness the party of officers became separated. At daylight, when Sherman reached the Salinas Plain, there were only two other officers accompanying him.

In the growing light they could see the tracks of the deserters. And as they rode forward, the sun rising ahead of them, they saw a cabin. There was a well in the yard with two men in army uniforms standing beside it.

The officers put their horses to a gallop. Sherman, who had the best horse, began to pull ahead. The men at the well were too busy drinking water and washing their faces to hear anything until Sherman was almost on them. Then, as they swung round, Sherman brought his horse to a halt, cocked his musket and leveled it at them. "Get in the cabin," he ordered.

For a moment the men hesitated. Sherman

37

raised the musket. Cursing softly, the men turned and went inside.

Sherman swung down from his horse and followed, musket at the ready. It held only one bullet, and the cabin was filled with men. Some were asleep on the floor, some eating food they had brought with them. "Stand up," Sherman ordered. "Face the wall." It was a foolhardy thing to do, confronting all these men with virtually no ammunition, but Sherman was counting on the authority of his rank.

Again the men hesitated. But now there was the sound of galloping horses outside. The soldiers had no way of knowing there were only two other officers; instead they believed Sherman must have brought an armed company with him. So they faced the wall and Sherman collected their pistols and muskets. He passed these to the two other officers who had now arrived. Then he marched the unarmed deserters outside.

By the time the men realized there were only three officers altogether, it was too late. With Sherman and his friends riding behind, the deserters were marched back across the plain to Monterey.

Not long after this Sherman was transferred to San Francisco, heart of the Gold Rush. Here arrived the ships from the east, crowded with would-be prospectors. And it was here that the prospectors returning from the mines brought their gold to be exchanged for supplies. The "horrid" village of Yerba Buena was now known as San Francisco and was growing by the hour. At this point it was even more horrid than it had been at Sherman's first visit. Telling about it later, he wrote:

"The rains were heavy, and the mud fearful. I have seen mules stumble in the street and drown in the liquid mud! Montgomery Street had been filled with brush and clay . . . the mud was so deep that a horse's legs would become entangled in the bushes below, and the rider was likely to be thrown and drowned in the mud. The only sidewalks were made of stepping stones of empty boxes. . . . Gambling was the chief occupation of the people. . . . Any room twenty by sixty feet would rent for a thousand dollars a month. I had as my pay seventy dollars a month, and no one would even try to hire a servant under three hundred."

Sherman's commanding officer realized that even with food furnished by the government his officers couldn't live on their pay. So whenever possible he gave them leave to take private positions. Sherman and his friend, Lieutenant Edward Ord, got jobs as surveyors.

It was while working on this job that, early one morning, the two lieutenants started to cross the upper end of San Francisco Bay in a small boat. They were a hundred yards or so offshore when they heard men shouting. Looking up, they saw men ashore running toward the beach and pointing at something in the bay.

"Over there!" Sherman said. "It's something swimming toward us."

Ord stared. "What kind of thing is it?"

"Let's go look."

They began to row toward the creature, which

continued to swim toward them. Sherman stood up to see better. "Look out!" he yelled at Ord. "That's a bear! A grizzly bear!"

A grizzly was the most powerful and dangerous animal in the West. Its jaws were large enough to crush a man's skull. With one blow of its paw it could break the back of a horse or upset a small boat. Swiftly Sherman grabbed his oar and he and Ord began to row hard, away from the bear toward a sailing ship anchored nearby. There were men watching from the ship's deck and Sherman began to shout, "Bear! Grizzly bear!"

One of the men on the ship rushed to his cabin and came back with a gun. He fired once, and the bear made a sound that was part growl, part howl. At the same time a large rowboat put out from the ship's side. In the bow stood a man with an ax.

As the boat came alongside, the bear made no effort to lunge for it. Instead it was using one paw to clutch at its jaw that had been struck by the bullet. Leaning forward, the man in the boat smashed his ax against the bear's head.

Later the bear's body was towed back to the ship. The carcass was skinned and cut into parts. Sherman and Ord took enough to eat for the next three days while surveying.

In two months' work as surveyors, the young lieutenants earned $12,000 between them. This was more than they would have made in seven years in the army. But when their two months' leave was over, they went back to army duty where Sherman had to use most of his $6,000 to meet expenses.

Not long after he received orders to go east.

5

Two Shipwrecks in One Day

Back in Washington, D.C., Sherman was told he would soon be promoted to captain. Now at last he and Ellen Ewing could be married. The wedding took place in Washington where Ellen's father was now the secretary of the interior. President Zachary Taylor himself came to the wedding, along with his entire cabinet and many famous congressmen.

With his new bride, Captain Sherman was sent to duty in St. Louis, Missouri. He was there only a short time, however, before being transferred to New Orleans. He liked New Orleans; he liked the Southern people here just as he had liked those in Charleston.

But there was one big problem. Even as a captain, Sherman's army pay was very small. His wife had always been accustomed to wealth. Although she truly loved Cump Sherman, she had been badly spoiled by her father and now she wanted Sherman to quit the army and go into business where he could make more money.

William Tecumseh Sherman

In his up-and-down moods Sherman had often talked about quitting the army; actually, however, he had never really wanted to quit. He felt that soldiering was the one job he knew, and he liked it. But when a friend offered to make him president of a bank in San Francisco, he felt it was his duty to his family to consider it. Even so he was cautious. He sent Ellen back to Lancaster, Ohio, took six months' leave from the army and went to California to investigate the job.

His ship, the *Lewis,* was supposed to reach San Francisco early on the morning of April 9, 1853. Before dawn, Sherman was asleep when he felt a terrible jolt that almost threw him out of his bunk. Moments later there was another crash, then another. Overhead he could hear men running and shouting at one another.

Quickly he went on deck. The night was dark, with fog so thick he could see only a few yards. He heard a sailor shout, "We've hit a reef!" There the ship stuck, but with each wave it would rise upward, then crash down again. Sherman realized that if this pounding kept up the ship might break in half.

By now passengers were all over the deck, some dressed, some half dressed. Women were screaming, babies crying. Several men, panic-stricken, tried to lower one of the lifeboats. They weren't sailors. Chances were they would have upset and lost the boat. But suddenly the ship's captain appeared out of the fog. He had a pistol in his hand. "Get away from that boat!" he ordered. The frightened men backed off.

42

"No boats will be lowered except by my orders and properly manned," the captain said.

Sherman watched the scene calmly. Danger excited him, but it was a kind of cold excitement in which his mind worked with great clarity. He knew the ship couldn't sink. It was already resting on the bottom. Eventually it might break in half, but that would take some time. So now he stood leaning against a bulkhead, watching the panic of the passengers. Occasionally he spoke to some lady who was particularly frightened, reassuring her that there was no immediate danger. He helped a mother with a scared baby. His own coolness helped to calm the people around him.

The ship's captain ordered one lifeboat lowered, manned by several sailors and an officer. It rowed off, disappearing into the fog. While it was gone the ship's bell kept ringing so the boat could find its way back.

When the lifeboat returned, the officer reported that land was only a short distance away. Now the other lifeboats were lowered. Women and children and some of the more frightened men climbed into them. They were taken ashore and the boats returned for more passengers.

Sherman was one of the last to leave the *Lewis*. On the beach he found all the ship's passengers huddled under a high bluff. They had built fires to dry their clothes, but otherwise no one seemed to be doing anything. "I know this country fairly well," Sherman said. "I think I can find my way to San Francisco and get help."

Away from the beach the country was hilly,

covered with grass and flowers. When he found the tracks of horses leading inland, he followed them until he came to a small river in which a boat was loading lumber from a sawmill.

"I'm just about to leave for San Francisco," the lumber boat's captain told Sherman. "I'll have you there by midafternoon."

But the day's adventure was not over yet. It was a small boat, top-heavy with the lumber piled on it. As the boat passed through the Golden Gate the wind increased sharply. The waves were suddenly choppy. One wave struck the boat broadside while a sudden gust of wind caught it. The boat rolled sharply. One gunwale went underwater and the other high in the air so that Sherman had to cling to the wheelhouse to keep from falling. For a long moment the boat hung on its side—then with a crash of loose timber rolled completely over.

Sherman was a good swimmer and so, fortunately, were the other three men on board. When the overturned boat continued to float upside down, the four men swam to it and climbed onto its bottom. "Two shipwrecks in one day," Sherman said, wiping the water out of his eyes, "is a little too much."

There was a chance this second wreck might prove more dangerous than the first. The tide was rapidly carrying the overturned craft out to sea. The waves were getting bigger. Sherman knew that any moment now the vessel might fill with water and sink to the bottom. Looking back at land he knew there was no chance to swim there against this rushing tide.

Suddenly he heard someone call, "That's a nice mess you've got yourselves into," and swinging around he saw a sailboat not fifty yards away. Quickly the shipwrecked men swam to it and were pulled aboard. Two hours later they were ashore in San Francisco and Sherman was sending help to the stranded passengers of the *Lewis*.

In the days following his two shipwrecks, Sherman investigated the possibilities of opening a new bank in San Francisco. The great gold rush of 1849 was over, but business was still good. He decided to take the new job, resigned from the army and brought his wife and the baby that had been born about a year before to California. A second child was soon to be born.

This was the start of the unhappiest years in Cump Sherman's life. Ellen did not like California. She would never like any place very much, except Lancaster, Ohio.

In all, the Shermans had five children, in quick succession, but the family was not very close. Except for this episode in the banking business, Sherman was a career officer. Like all professional officers, he would spend years away from home, particularly during wars. And his wife was an army wife, often left alone, taking care of the children but also spending a great deal of time with her father, either in Lancaster or in Washington, D.C.

In San Francisco, Sherman's health wasn't good, and he nervously smoked one cigar after another. This had never bothered him much so long as most of his work was outdoors, but working in a bank he began to suffer from asthma.

To make matters worse, business soon began to go bad. Sherman himself proved to be an excellent banker. His own bank did not fail, but many others in San Francisco did. When he had been in California four years, the bank owners decided to close it. They gave Sherman another job, this time in New York City. This job lasted only a short time before the company went out of business altogether.

Now Sherman was out of work. Not only that, while he was in California several friends had asked him to invest money for them. He had invested it honestly, but in the general depression some of the money had been lost. Sherman wasn't responsible. Still, his own father had once assumed the debts of men who worked for him, and Cump insisted on doing the same. Now he used all the money he had ever saved trying to pay back what his friends had lost.

This made Ellen furious. "This isn't your responsibility!" she told him angrily. "You're paying these men with money that your own family needs. You're taking it from me, and from our children!"

He didn't answer, because there was no answer. It was true that his own family needed money. They always needed money. Yet deep inside himself Cump's sense of honor demanded that he repay what had been lost and he felt like some animal caught in a trap from which there is no escape until the hunter comes to kill it.

Without money and without work, Sherman's mood was one of total despair. Always given to extremes, he saw things as worse than they were. Away from home, looking for work, he wrote Ellen,

"I am doomed to be a vagabond and shall no longer struggle against my fate. . . . I look upon myself as a dead cock in the pit, not worthy of further notice. . . ."

One day in St. Louis he saw a bearded, dirty little man driving a wagon along the street, selling wood from house to house. For a moment he stared at the man, trying to remember where he had seen him before. And then he remembered. It was U. S. Grant with whom he had gone to West Point!

At the same time, Grant turned and saw Sherman. Neither man really wanted to talk to the other, but there was no way of avoiding it. "I quit the army," Grant said. "Now I have a little farm outside town." He didn't mention that it really belonged to his wife, that he himself had lost one job after another until there was nothing left for him except to live on his wife's farm. "What are you doing?" he asked Cump Sherman.

"I'm out of the army, too. I was president of a bank in California for awhile, until the owners decided to close it." He added quickly, "It didn't fail. Nobody lost any money in it."

They talked briefly, unhappily, both ashamed to admit failure but too honest to deny it. Finally Grant climbed back on his wagon; Sherman walked on down the street. A few years later, U. S. Grant and Tecumseh Sherman would help change the fate of a nation, but the autumn of 1858 was a low point in both their lives. As he continued on, Sherman told himself bitterly, "West Point and the regular army aren't good schools for farmers and bankers."

6

The War Begins

When life looked blackest for Tecumseh Sherman, he suddenly got the offer of a good job. The state of Louisiana was building a new military school to be called the Louisiana State Seminary of Learning and Military Academy (many years later it would be known as Louisiana State University). Sherman was asked to be the first superintendent.

Leaving Ellen and his large family (by now, five children) in Lancaster, Sherman went south to start the new school. It opened on January 1, 1860, with sixty cadets, and from the first Sherman was happy with his work.

And yet there was also a problem. For many years now the question of slavery had divided the North and South with increasing bitterness. By 1860 many people in the South were saying the Southern states ought to secede from the Union and start their own nation.

Cump Sherman considered this to be treason. He still had no strong feelings about slavery. But

48

from early childhood on he had never forgotten the sentiments of his foster-father, Thomas Ewing, who had impressed on him time and again that the Union was sacred.

Sherman's closest friend at the Academy was Professor David Boyd. Boyd was from Virginia, and he and Sherman had long, intense but friendly arguments about secession. "Now look here," Boyd said once, "do you really believe that if the Southern states secede from the Union, there will be a war?"

"I do."

"Well, I don't," Boyd said. "I've heard a dozen people, important people, say, 'A lady's thimble will hold all the blood to be shed over this.' They say the North won't fight."

"They don't know what they're talking about," Sherman insisted. "The Mississippi River rises in the North. The people in the North have got to be able to send their produce down the Mississippi. They can't allow another country to control the mouth of the river. Thomas Jefferson knew this when he bought the Louisiana Territory from France."

"But if the South wants to secede and set up its own country, what right has the North to interfere?" Boyd asked.

"Because the Union must be preserved," Sherman said. "If the Southern states have a right to secede from the Union, then, of course, they would have the right to secede from one another. The cotton-growing states along the Gulf would soon have trouble with the others, like Virginia and Tennessee. Then Tennessee and Virginia might se-

49

cede. Florida and Georgia might argue about their border, and Florida secede, to become a country of its own. Or counties might even secede from states. We would soon have a hundred tiny countries, with wars going on between them all the time."

So the two men argued, still admiring and respecting one another. But across the nation as a whole, most people could not remain so calm. Slave owners in the South said the North wanted to abolish slavery and ruin the economy of the South. Abolitionists in the North said slavery was evil and should be destroyed. If this ruined the South, they said, it was the South's own fault. One thing that made Sherman's position in Louisiana even more difficult was the fact that his brother John was now a congressman from Ohio and one of the leading Abolitionists.

In November 1860 Abraham Lincoln was elected President. People in the South knew Lincoln was opposed to slavery. Although he would not actually take office until March 1861, the talk of secession grew hotter than ever.

On Christmas Eve of 1860, Cump Sherman and David Boyd were alone in Sherman's office. The school was closed for the holidays and all the students had gone home. The big frame building was strangely quiet as Sherman opened some newspapers that had just arrived. The mails were very slow, and all the papers were several days old. He opened one dated December 20, 1860. The headline blazed at him:

SOUTH CAROLINA SECEDES!

For a long while Sherman stared at the paper without moving, without seeming to breathe. Tears came to his eyes. They moved in slow drops down his cheeks. He had known for a long time this was going to happen, and yet he had hoped against hope.

Professor Boyd looked up from his paper and saw the tears on Sherman's cheeks. "Cump," he said, "what—?"

"South Carolina has seceded."

For a moment the two friends, one from the North, one from the South, looked at each other. "It was bound to happen," Boyd said finally. "But it doesn't necessarily mean war."

Sherman hurled the newspaper from him. He leaped up and began to pace back and forth across the room. "You people in the South," he cried. "You think you can have peaceful secession! You can't! You don't know what you are doing! You are forcing a war that will drench this nation in blood."

Boyd did not answer. He had never seen his friend in such a frenzy. "The Union must be preserved," Sherman said. His voice was choking. "I will have to fight against you, against your people —the people I love best in all this country."

He turned, almost stumbling, and crossed the room to stand looking out the window. It was a view he had always loved—a long, gently sloping hill covered with tall pines. When he spoke again it was almost as if he were seeing a vision. It impressed Professor Boyd so much that later he tried to write it all down.

"You mistake the people in the North," Sherman said hoarsely. "They are a peaceable people, but they will fight too, and they aren't going to let this country be destroyed without a mighty effort to save it.

"Besides, the Northern people greatly outnumber the whites in the South. And they are a mechanical people. They not only manufacture guns and ammunition, the weapons of war, they make steam engines, ships, railroads. You in the South are agriculturists. Even the shoes and clothing you wear are made in the North."

He turned away from the window. He sat down at his desk and covered his red-bearded face with both hands. "You may win a few battles at first," he said. "But as your resources give out, you will start to lose. And it will be a long war, a terrible, bloody war." His voice broke. When he spoke next it was barely a whisper, "If your people would only stop and think. . . ."

But Southern politicians were in no mood for thinking. One state after another followed South Carolina out of the Union. The Louisiana legislature was to meet January 25. Sherman knew it would vote to secede. On January 18 he wrote to the governor of Louisiana.

> *Sir:*
>
> *As I occupy a quasi-military position under the laws of the State, I deem it proper to acquaint you that I accepted such a position when Louisiana was a state in the Union and when the motto of this Seminary was inserted*

in marble over the main door: "By the liberality of the general government of the United States. The Union—esto perpetua."

Recent events foreshadow a great change and it becomes all men to choose. If Louisiana withdraws from the Federal Union, I prefer to maintain my allegiance to the constitution so long as a fragment of it survives and my longer stay here would be wrong in every sense of the word.

. . . I beg you to take immediate steps to relieve me as Superintendent the moment the State determines to secede, for on no earthly account will I do any act or think any thought hostile or in defiance to the old government of the United States."

Reluctantly the governor of Louisiana accepted Sherman's resignation and wrote him: "You cannot regret more than I do the necessity which deprives us of your services, and you bear with you the respect, confidence, and admiration of all who have been associated with you."

To Sherman's surprise, the war did not start as promptly as he had expected. James Buchanan was still President, and even when the Southern states set up their own government, with Jefferson Davis as their President, Buchanan took no action.

On March 4, 1861, Lincoln moved into the White House. And still there was no action taken against the South. Sherman could not understand this. His brother John, the congressman, was living in Washington and Cump went to visit him. Together they called on President Lincoln. Still sure that war must begin soon, Cump planned to ask Lincoln for reappointment to the army.

"Mr. President," John Sherman said, "this is my brother who is just up from Louisiana. He may give you some information you want."

"Ah," said Lincoln, "how are they getting along down there?"

"They think they are getting along swimmingly," Cump answered. "They are preparing for war."

Lincoln shrugged his wide, bony shoulders. "Oh, well. I guess we'll manage to keep house."

The answer made Cump Sherman furious. He had come hoping he could make Lincoln understand the need for action. But the tall, homely man didn't even seem interested.

Lincoln of course had good reasons for delaying action against the South. His determination to save the Union never wavered. But he was waiting for the proper time to move. He knew that many people in the North didn't want war and that these people wouldn't support a war they believed had been forced on them by the federal government. Lincoln also realized that such border states as Maryland, Kentucky and Missouri might join the South if the North precipitated a conflict. And so he waited.

Sherman was too impatient to consider these points. He never had much patience with or understanding of politics. Both his brother John and his foster-father were important politicians. Cump could, and did, love and respect them. But nonetheless he felt only contempt for politics and politicians

54

in general. Angrily he left Washington, went to St. Louis and took a job as head of a small streetcar company.

It wasn't for long. On April 12, 1861, the South attacked the Union's Fort Sumter in Charleston, South Carolina. Immediately a wave of patriotism swept the North. Men, who a day before had not thought the Union worth fighting for, were furious at being attacked. The South had started the war, and now the North was ready to fight back.

This was the mood Lincoln had been waiting for. He called for 75,000 men to volunteer for three months. Sherman knew the war couldn't be won in three months, and waited. Then Lincoln called for men to volunteer for three years' service.

Quickly Sherman volunteered. On May 14, 1861, he was appointed colonel of the 13th Regular Infantry. It meant leaving his family for an indefinite length of time, but he would regularly write to Ellen, and he knew that she would always have great moral support from her father.

7

The Battle of Bull Run

The new Union army assembled near Washington —and a strange outfit it was. Some of the men wore the blue uniform of the regular army. But there weren't enough blue uniforms to go around, and some wore the uniforms of state militia: blue or green or brown, with at least one regiment dressed in gray very much like that of the Confederate army. Many of the men had no guns. And almost none of them knew anything about military drill or discipline.

Colonel Cump Sherman's first job was to try to turn a happy-go-lucky crowd of young men into a well-knit military organization. Given enough time he would have succeeded. But there wasn't enough time. All over the North newspaper editors were writing that the Union army ought to move rapidly. One quick battle, they said, and the North could capture Richmond and end the war.

Politicians were making the same kind of speeches. "What's the matter with the army?" they asked, and demanded: "Capture Richmond. Get the war over with!"

Cump Sherman was always quick to anger, and this kind of talk made him furious. "There's nothing wrong with the army that a little time and training won't take care of," he told a friend. "It's these crazy politicians and newspaper reporters who are wrong. If we send an untrained army to attack Richmond, we'll be sending them to their deaths."

But the politicians and newspapers kept insisting. The Southern army was no better trained than the Northern army, they said. And the North already had more men under arms. Soon all over the North people were shouting, "On to Richmond!" President Lincoln gave the order. With barely two weeks of training the army folded its tents and headed south.

About thirty miles away, encamped along the south bank of a little Virginia stream called Bull Run, the Confederate army lay waiting.

Completely without discipline, the Union soldiers were more like a mob on the way to some giant picnic than a trained army on the march. Sherman rode up and down the line trying to keep order, but it was impossible. The men broke ranks to run into nearby fields and gather blackberries. Because they were in Rebel territory, they felt free to steal the Virginia farmers' pigs and chickens.

Cump Sherman was coldly angry at his own men. He knew that many Southerners had not wanted to leave the Union. He had hoped that good discipline and the offer of friendship would win these people away from the South. And he knew that the moblike actions of the army made enemies rather than friends. Later he wrote Ellen: "No curse could be greater than the invasion of a volunteer army. No Goths or Vandals ever had less respect for the lives and property of friends and foes, and henceforth we ought never to hope for any friends in Virginia."

Near the little town of Centreville the head of the Union army halted and waited for the rest to catch up. Bull Run Creek was only three miles away. One Union brigade was sent forward to cross it at a place called Blackburn's Ford to test the strength of the Confederate lines.

Sherman wasn't with the men who went forward, but from where he waited at Centreville he heard the guns begin to fire. It was the first time he had ever heard artillery in action against an enemy. As he listened, the firing grew heavier.

Suddenly an officer on horseback galloped up and handed him a message. It was from General Daniel Tyler. The brigade had met stiff opposition and was being thrown back. Sherman was to take his own brigade forward as rapidly as possible to cover the retreat of the other.

At double-quick time Sherman's men trotted down the long dirt road. Sherman rode with them. Most of the time he kept his horse off the road so as not to interfere with the trotting men. The firing was closer now.

Coming over the crest of a low hill, Cump Sherman saw Bull Run Creek ahead. Men in blue uniforms were splashing through the water, running back toward the Union side. Artillery shells fell among them. An officer on horseback vanished in a great brown geyser of creek water.

Sherman halted his own brigade. Riding up and down, he got his men into battle line. The men in blue were running up the hill toward him now, but no Confederates were visible in the woods beyond the creek.

Artillery shells followed the Union forces up the hill. Suddenly they began to burst near the men on the crest.

It was the first time Sherman had been under fire in battle. Like every soldier, he had wondered what his reactions would be. Now he felt much as he had when his ship was wrecked off the California coast—he was excited, but his mind kept working clearly, precisely. He knew that he was in danger. He felt fear. But he could control it, push it away and get on with his work.

The Confederates did not cross the creek. Instead, the firing stopped. And Sherman, following orders, withdrew his own men to Centreville.

This fight on July 18, 1861, was little more than a skirmish. The big battle of Bull Run came three days later. As Sherman himself would later say, it was one of the best-planned and worst-fought battles of the whole war.

General Irwin McDowell, who commanded the Union army, and General Pierre Beauregard, who commanded the Confederate army, had been classmates at West Point. They had been taught the same military tactics. Now, with the two armies facing each other, their plans were almost identical.

Each general planned to make a small, frontal attack against the middle of the enemy line; then he would swing the main body of his army to the right and strike the big blow against the enemy flank.

Had the plans of both generals been put into operation at the same time, the two armies might have gone around in a circle, leaving the Confederate army free to march on Washington and the Union army with an open road to Richmond.

It didn't work out that way. The Union army moved first. Starting shortly after midnight on July 21, part of it marched down the road that led from Centreville to a stone bridge over Bull Run. The bulk of the army circled off to the right, planning to cross Bull Run a mile or two to the west.

Sherman's brigade went with the men moving straight toward the stone bridge. There was a full moon dipping low in the west. The weather had been dry for weeks and pale spurts of dust rose beneath the hoofs of Sherman's horse. Dust formed in a low cloud over the marching men. Then, just before reaching the stone bridge, they turned off the road and stopped beneath some trees. Here they were to wait for further orders.

They waited for hours. Sherman knew that the untrained divisions circling to the right were taking far too long to get into position, but his orders were to wait. While his men loafed, Sherman rode back and forth between them and the creek. Carefully he studied the landscape, fixing it in his mind. Once he saw a Confederate officer ride down a steep bank on the far side of the creek, wade his horse across

60

and look toward the Union troops. Then the officer rode back across the creek.

Sherman fixed the spot in his mind. According to his map, the water here was too deep for a man to wade across. But if the horse had been able to wade, then a man could.

About ten o'clock firing began near the stone

bridge. Then off to the right guns began to boom. The firing to the right became heavier. And still Sherman and his men waited.

It was noon when an officer galloped up with orders. Sherman was to take his brigade and join the men fighting on the right.

Now Sherman remembered the horseman he had seen cross the creek. Instead of circling several miles to the right as the main army had done, he waded his men through the creek where the Confederate horseman had crossed. On the far side was a steep bluff. The infantry climbed it without trouble, but the artillery could not get up. Sherman marched on without his big guns. The firing to the right was growing heavier and closer. By the sound of it he judged that the Confederates were retreating and that his advance would bring him to the flank of the Southern force.

Ahead of him was a thin stand of pine trees. As he moved forward, Sherman saw men in gray running through the trees. They were going toward his left, retreating from the fight and now and then stopping to fire to their rear.

Without orders one of Sherman's officers sent his horse dashing forward. Perhaps he thought he was leading a charge. Perhaps he thought the scattered Confederates would surrender at the mere sight of him. Instead, several Rebels raised their guns. There was the crash of gunfire, and the officer fell from his horse.

Now one of Sherman's regiments began to fire, but the main fight was off to the right and ahead. Sherman ordered his men to move toward it.

At the sight of Sherman's brigade coming up on their flank, the main Southern defense broke. Firing, then running back a few steps, firing again, running again, the Confederates retreated down the slope of a long hill.

It was early afternoon now. The sun blazed down, blurred by the low-hanging clouds of smoke and dust. The heat was terrible. There was a small brook at the foot of the hill, and some of the retreating Confederates stopped to drink from it. Some fell dead at the spot, their blood staining the water.

The Confederates retreated up the next hill. It was almost a rout now, men running without stopping to fire. The Northern soldiers pushed hard after them. But Confederate artillery was dropping shells among the Union soldiers with deadly effect.

On the far side of the hill an event was taking place that would add a new name and a new hero to American history. A bearded, deeply religious Confederate general named Thomas Jackson had just arrived with a brigade of fresh troops. He had stationed them a little back from the crest of the hill with a clear field of fire ahead of them. Here they stood steady, waiting for the Union attack. Fleeing Confederates ran past them on both sides. Confederate General Barnard Bee was trying to stop them. Riding his horse among the running men he shouted, "Look! There is Jackson standing like a stone wall. Rally behind the Virginians!"

The running men stopped. By twos and threes and tens they did rally behind Jackson's force. And forever afterward Thomas Jonathan Jackson would be called Stonewall Jackson.

On the other side of the hill Colonel Sherman led his men forward. He had found a road leading up the hill between high banks that offered protection from the Southern guns. But beyond the crest of the hill there was only open country. And the men coming up the road could attack across it only one unit at a time.

The men went forward bravely enough. But they went straight into Jackson's fire, backed up by the men who had rallied behind him. Confederate artillery battered them. One after another Sherman's regiments attacked—one after another they were beaten back.

Again and again Sherman rallied his men where the hill gave some protection. In the excitement he had forgotten his fear. A bullet scratched his shoulder. Another ripped through his trousers at the knee. He hardly noticed.

One of Colonel Sherman's regiments, the Wisconsin 2nd, wore gray uniforms much like those of the Confederates. Beaten back from the crest of the hill, they were fired on by their own men before Sherman could prevent it. In the terrible confusion men began to break and run as fast as the Confederates had done an hour or two before.

Sherman managed to hold most of his men together, but around him other regiments were falling apart completely. Some men dropped their guns in order to run faster, shouting that the battle was lost. This frightened others still fighting.

Sherman's brigade was one of the last to retreat, still with some organization, still fighting. It went back across Bull Run, out of range of the enemy now, and on to Centreville. General McDowell had given orders for the army to rally there and continue the battle the next day.

It was too late. One of the strangest situations in American history had helped turn the retreat of the Union army into a total rout.

Before the battle many people from Washington had driven south in buggies and carriages. They thought it would be fun to watch a battle. Like a vast crowd of picnickers they had spread out along the road and over the fields near Bull Run. When they saw the Union soldiers retreating, panic seized them and they began to race toward Washington. Buggies overturned, blocking the road and the bridges. Soldiers caught the terror of the civilians like a fever. The army fell apart. Even Sherman's brigade became an unruly mob of men running toward Washington.

All during the night he rode back and forth, trying to bring order out of chaos. But it wasn't until the men reached the Potomac River that they began to rally.

Sherman expected the Confederate army to follow. Had it done so, it might possibly have captured Washington. But the truth was, the Confederate army had been almost as badly battered as the Union. And the men were just as undisciplined. As a result the Confederates were in no condition to attack.

Now both armies, exhausted, took time out to lick their wounds and reorganize.

8

"General William T. Sherman Insane"

Colonel Sherman was deeply troubled by the Union defeat at Bull Run. Before the encounter he had warned against sending untrained men into battle. Now he blamed the newspapers and the politicians who had shouted "On to Richmond!" for what had happened. He wrote bitterly to his wife, "Courage our people have, but no government."

The defeat at Bull Run had badly shaken the confidence of the volunteers. Many began to desert. Once Sherman ordered a battery of his regular army artillery to stand ready to fire on one of their own units if the men tried to leave camp. Many soldiers who had volunteered to serve for only three months began to claim their time was up, whether it was or not. All this added to the terrible strain of trying to train and discipline men for the next battle. Several weeks after Bull Run, Sherman wrote to his brother John: "I have not undressed a night since . . . and the volunteers will not allow of sleep by day."

It was at this time that one of Sherman's officers strolled up to him in front of a group of enlisted men and said casually, "Colonel, I'm going to New York today. Is there anything I can do for you?"

For a moment Sherman could only stare. Then he said, "Did I sign an order for you to leave camp?"

The officer laughed. "No. But I volunteered to serve three months. My time is up. So I'm leaving."

The enlisted men were listening closely. Sherman knew that if he let this officer leave camp, about half his men would desert also. "Captain," he said, "the question of your time of service has been submitted to the proper authorities." His voice was steady, and loud enough for the other men to hear him clearly. "The decision to hold volunteers in camp has been published in orders. You know this. You are a soldier, and will obey orders." His voice was louder now. "If you try to leave without orders, I will shoot you like a dog. Now go back to your post."

The captain's face went white with anger. But after a moment he obeyed.

Later that same day an orderly ran into Sherman's tent to tell him that President Lincoln had arrived in camp. Hurrying out, Sherman found the President in a carriage with Secretary of State William Seward. "We heard you'd got the boys over their big scare at Bull Run," Lincoln said, "and thought we'd visit to see how things are going. Ride with us."

Sherman got into the carriage. "Mr. President," he asked, "are you going to speak to the troops?"

"I'd like to."

Bluntly Sherman said, "I hope you won't encourage any wild shouting and cheering, Mr. President. We had enough hurrahing and that sort of thing before Bull Run to spoil any man. What we need now are sober truths and hard work."

The President turned his homely face to him. After a moment he said, "Very well, Colonel. I think I know what you mean."

The carriage stopped in the middle of the camp and men gathered around quickly. President Lincoln stood up to speak. He talked about the duty of the men to their country, the defeat that was past, the hope for victory in the future. "Don't cheer, boys," he said. "I confess I rather like it myself. But Colonel Sherman says it's not military, and I guess we'd better defer to his opinion."

At this point the captain whom Sherman had spoken to in the morning pushed his way through the crowd. Sherman saw him coming and knew there would be trouble. In his speech Lincoln had said if the men had complaints about unjust treatment they could tell him about them.

"Mr. President," the captain called, "I have a

complaint. This morning I spoke to Colonel Sherman and he threatened to shoot me."

There was a sudden quiet. Everyone waited for the President's answer.

"Threatened to shoot you?" Lincoln said. He glanced at Sherman sitting perfectly motionless in the carriage. Then he looked back at the captain. He leaned forward, put one hand beside his mouth and said in a loud whisper, "Well, if I were you and he threatened to shoot, I wouldn't trust him. Because I believe he'd do it!"

Soldiers standing nearby howled with laughter. The captain's face grew red, and he slunk away.

As the carriage drove on Sherman explained what had happened that morning. Lincoln nodded. "Of course, I didn't know anything about it," he said. "But I thought you knew your business best."

After their first meeting, Cump Sherman had not liked Abraham Lincoln. But from that day on he had more respect for the tall, rangy man who bore more burdens of government than any soldier, no matter how high his rank, could conceive of.

Not long after this Sherman was promoted to brigadier general. At about the same time General Robert Anderson, who commanded the Union troops in Kentucky, asked that Sherman be made his second in command.

Cump was glad to serve under his old friend. However, not long after he reached Kentucky, General Anderson became ill. This left Sherman in command, and at that time in his life he was terrified of being a commanding officer. Perhaps he felt that he wasn't yet ready to command an army.

Perhaps he still didn't trust the President, the politicians in Washington, the way the war was being fought. He never made his reasons fully clear, and it may be that he himself did not completely understand them.

Whatever his reasons, Sherman became the commanding officer in Kentucky against his will. But like a good soldier he accepted the job and did his best even while asking to be relieved.

It was a difficult job. Sherman was responsible for a front that extended from West Virginia in the east to Missouri in the west. Yet he had very few soldiers, and practically all of them were volunteers with no experience. A huge Union army was being gathered outside Washington, another large army in Missouri. Both these armies were larger than Sherman's although they had less territory to cover.

After Bull Run he had worked long hours with little sleep. In Kentucky he worked even harder, training the men he had and trying to get more troops sent to his command. If he had slept little after Bull Run, now he slept almost not at all. Instead of waiting for messages to be brought to his headquarters, he went, early each night, to the telegraph station in Louisville.

There he paced up and down, smoking one cigar after another, grabbing the telegrams as fast as the operator could write them down. When the telegraph office closed at two in the morning he went back to his quarters in a hotel. But instead of sleeping, he walked up and down the hotel corridors smoking and thinking. People began to stare at him, whispering that he was just a little strange.

Absorbed as he was in his work, Cump Sherman did indeed do some strange absentminded things. Sometimes he wore an old top hat along with his uniform. Once while inspecting an outpost he finished the cigar he had been smoking, threw it away and put another in his mouth. He groped in his pockets for a match, found none and asked an officer nearby for a light. The officer, who had just lit a cigar of his own, handed it to him. Sherman used it to light his own cigar. Then, deep in thought, he threw away the officer's cigar, oblivious to the latter's amusement.

Sherman worked his men almost as hard as he worked himself. "He's a bitter pill to take," one soldier told another. Soon the men began to call him "Old Pills."

Yet, hard as he worked his men, it was obvious that he did this to make them better soldiers. One day he was bawling out a soldier for some poorly done job when suddenly he stopped. He blinked, as though he were seeing the man in front of him clearly for the first time, and said, "I understand you men are short of rations."

"Yes, sir."

"Well, wait here a minute." He went to a nearby commissary, brought back an armful of food and gave it to the soldier. It was after several acts of this kind that some of the men changed his nickname from "Old Pills" to "Sugarcoated."

To add to Sherman's worries, Kentucky was a border state in which many people favored the Confederacy. In his exhausted, strained condition, and always given to moods, he began to think

Kentucky might join the South. Actually twice as many Kentuckians were joining the Union army as were joining the Southern army. But Sherman wrote to Washington saying things were just the other way around. He began to believe wild stories about the strength of the Southern army. Time after time he reported to Washington that the Confederates were about to capture Louisville and sweep through Kentucky.

Eventually Simon Cameron, the secretary of war, visited General Sherman to get a firsthand report on the situation. Sherman told him that just to hold Kentucky he would need 60,000 men. Then he outlined the plan that had been in his mind from the first. To end the war, he said, the Union army should drive south from Kentucky, capture the key points along the Mississippi River and cut the Confederacy in two. "Whoever controls the Mississippi," he told Cameron, "will win the war."

Secretary Cameron was far more interested in the armies in the east around Washington than in those in the west. Casually he asked, "How many men will you need?"

Perhaps Cameron was still talking about Sherman's present needs to hold Kentucky, but Sherman thought he meant how many would be needed to capture the key points along the Mississippi River. "Two hundred thousand," he replied.

The secretary of war jumped. "Great God!" he cried. "Where are they to come from?"

"It is the job of the government to raise troops," Sherman answered.

When Secretary Cameron returned to Washington he wrote a report in which he referred to Sherman's "insane request" for 200,000 men. A newspaperman who disliked Sherman saw this and wrote a story in which he hinted that General Sherman was crazy.

Sherman had never liked newspapers or reporters. He had made many enemies among them, often refusing to talk with representatives of the press. Now the papers began to get even. One reporter wrote:

> When I first saw him . . . his eyes had a half wild expression, probably the result of excessive smoking. . . . Sometimes he works for twenty consecutive hours. He sleeps little; nor do the most powerful opiates relieve his terrible cerebral excitement. Indifferent to dress and fare, he can live on bread and water, and fancies anyone else can do so.

Another paper wrote that General Anderson, who had been in command before Sherman, "was a gentleman of no mind. Sherman is possessed of neither mind nor manners."

Another paper ran a headline—GENERAL WILLIAM T. SHERMAN INSANE—and referred to him as "stark mad."

Sherman was relieved of his command and sent home to rest. He knew that he was not insane, but he felt disgraced. He believed his army career was at an end. He was so depressed that it is said that for a brief while he actually thought of killing himself.

9

The Battle of Shiloh Church

Sherman had less than a month's leave from
the army. Yet in that short time, with plenty of rest
and no troops to worry about, his entire mood began
to change. Taken care of by his wife, surrounded
by his children, he became more cheerful. He
realized that he had overestimated the strength of
the Confederate army and the danger to his own
men. He made up his mind that in the future he
would weigh gossip, information and misinforma-
tion more carefully in an effort to establish the truth.
But he still was reluctant to assume the responsibility of a large, independent command.

His first assignment after his leave was the
recruiting and training of new soldiers. One day, in
a small town in Iowa, the new recruits had just
lined up when the mother of one of them came
rushing up, threw her arms around her son and
began to weep. "Darby's not old enough to be a
soldier!" she cried. "I won't let him go to war!"

Two months before, such an incident might

have upset the high-strung Sherman. Now he thought it was merely amusing. "Madam," he said politely but firmly, "your son is seventeen years old. He has sworn it himself. He's in the army and will have to stay."

"Darby's my baby!" the woman shouted. She clung to the boy whose face was red with embarrassment. "I don't want him to leave home!"

"If he stays," Sherman said, "everyone will think he's a coward, or a mama's boy. Do you want that?"

The woman hesitated. Darby was trying to wriggle out of her grasp saying, "Aw, Mama, I'm growed up now. I'm growed!"

"If he goes with me," Sherman said, "Darby may be a hero when he comes home."

Slowly the woman released her grip on the boy. "All right," she said. "Darby, you stay close to the general and don't get hurt."

"Yes, Mama," Darby said. And, still red-faced, he marched off with the other men.

While Sherman was training soldiers near St. Louis, General U. S. Grant led a Union force up the Tennessee River to capture the Confederate Fort Henry. Then Grant took Fort Donelson on the Cumberland River. (Grant, whom Sherman had met on the streets in St. Louis, had rejoined the army at the start of the war, with the rank of colonel. He was soon promoted to brigadier general.)

With Fort Donelson in Union hands, Sherman was ordered to take troops up the Tennessee River on gunboats to somewhere near the Mississippi-

Alabama border. Here he was to land, move across country and destroy part of the Memphis & Charleston Railroad. This was one of the most important railroads in the South and the destruction of it would be a hard blow to the Confederacy.

Sherman moved rapidly. His gunboats churned southward—which was upstream on the Tennessee. But now, in the early spring of 1862, he was surrounded by swamps. Rain poured down and the flood was still rising. He realized that if he pushed on his men would soon be unable to return to their gunboats and might be drowned in the rising waters.

A few months before, Cump Sherman might have considered his inability to cut the railroad a personal disgrace. Now he merely accepted the fact that the weather prevented him from reaching his goal and ordered his men back to the gunboats.

Sherman took his men back downstream to a place called Pittsburg Landing that had high bluffs well above the flood. The place had two or three old warehouses and beyond them great orchards of peach trees in early bloom. From a point on the west bank a dirt road ran southwest toward the city of Corinth, Mississippi. Near this road, about two miles from the river, sat a small log church called the Shiloh Meeting House. Sherman pitched his tent near the church and his men camped around him. His orders were to wait there until he was joined by General Grant and Grant's army.

Meanwhile General Albert Sidney Johnston was gathering a Confederate army at Corinth, only thirty miles away. Johnston's second in command was General Pierre Beauregard, the same officer who had once sat with Sherman before an open fire at West Point talking about slavery.

One of the greatest battles of the entire Civil War was in the making.

A few days after Sherman made camp near Shiloh Meeting House, General Grant arrived with his army. This put Grant in command of the entire Union force of which Sherman commanded one division. Grant's plan was to march southwest to Corinth and destroy the Memphis & Charleston Railroad at that point. But before beginning his march he waited for General Don Carlos Buell to arrive with more troops.

At Corinth the scouts of General Johnston were keeping him informed of Grant's movements. Johnston knew that Grant's army was about the same size as his own, but it would be far bigger once it joined with the forces of General Buell. Johnston decided to strike at Grant before Buell's reinforcements could arrive.

On Thursday, April 3, 1862, the Confederates marched out of Corinth and started toward Pittsburg Landing, thirty miles away.

Both armies were made up largely of green troops who had never been under fire. Uniforms were still a wild mixture of colors and styles. Many of the Confederates had never been issued muskets and merely carried the shotguns with which they had gone hunting back home. A few had no guns at all but wore knives in their belts. There was little discipline. On Thursday, when it started to rain, many of the soldiers broke ranks to take refuge in

barns and houses. Units became mixed. By night-
fall most of the soldiers had gone only a few miles,
and neither Johnston nor Beauregard knew where
many of them were.

Friday was equally bad. The Confederates were
supposed to be slipping up on the Union forces to
take them by surprise. But it was Saturday night
before the Confederate army covered most of the
thirty miles between Corinth and Pittsburg Landing. They then cooked their food over fires visible
to Union pickets through the pines.

Around one of these fires the Confederate leaders met. General Beauregard wanted to call off the
attack. "The way our troops have been blundering
along," he said, "there is absolutely no chance of
surprise. The Union forces are every bit as strong
as we are. They are in a spot that can be easily
defended. And by now they must have built strong
fortifications."

General Johnston was determined to go ahead.
"Our troops are without experience and without
discipline," he said. "If we lead them here, believing
they're going to attack the Yankees, then retreat
without a fight, many of them will simply walk off
and go home. We're likely to get back to Corinth
minus an army."

Johnston won the discussion. After the decision to fight had been made, Beauregard turned to
the other officers and said, "Gentlemen, we shall
sleep tomorrow night in the enemy camp."

Some five miles away, General Sherman was
making a routine inspection of his own men.
Strange as it may seem, neither Sherman nor Grant

had any idea that a large Confederate army lay just few miles away, waiting for dawn.

It was true that for two days Union pickets had been reporting the movement of Southern troops, but Sherman believed these were merely scouting parties. As a commanding officer in Kentucky he had believed the wildest of rumors about enemy strength. Now he wasn't going to make that mistake again. Even as the Confederates were forming their battle line late on Saturday afternoon he told General Grant, "I don't expect anything like an attack on our position." And Grant agreed with him.

But at dawn on Sunday, April 6, the Confederates did attack.

It was not a sudden, massive advance. The young, inexperienced troops moved forward in scattered columns. Ahead of them went a line of skirmishers carrying their guns like quail hunters. The sun was barely up and the trees made long, dew-wet shadows.

Here and there a Yankee picket, hunched against the early morning chill, came suddenly wide awake as he saw the advancing skirmishers, fired at them and raced back to report what he had seen. As the skirmish line advanced the firing grew more widespread. But it was still scattered—two or three shots here, three or four a quarter of a mile away.

A little before seven o'clock Sherman was eating breakfast in his tent. He could hear shots in the distance, but there had been activity along the line for several days and he paid little attention.

79

A courier entered. "I'm from Colonel Jesse Appler, sir. Colonel Appler reports strong Rebel forces are driving back our pickets."

Sherman didn't even put down his fork. He knew Colonel Appler was a man easily frightened; for several days he had been sending wild reports about Confederate troops. "Go back and tell the colonel you fellows must be badly scared over there," Sherman said and kept on eating.

But the firing continued. It grew louder and more general. Sherman walked outside his tent to listen. His staff had gathered around him now. "Let's ride out and take a look," he said.

He rode at a trot to Appler's camp. Here the colonel had had the long roll sounded on the drums and his men were in battle line. But there was no sign of Confederate troops. Sherman rode on to where an open field sloped downward to a small stream lined by bushes, with bigger trees beyond it. He halted his horse and with field glasses began to examine the woods beyond the stream.

A flickering line of fire glittered along the edge of the bushes. Seconds later came the crash of muskets. And beside Sherman one of his orderlies, Thomas Holliday of the 2nd Illinois Cavalry, fell dead from his horse.

Again guns crackled from the line of bushes beside the stream. Sherman's staff quickly gathered around him. "General, you've got to get away from here!" one of them shouted.

They rode back up the slope, a little beyond musket range. Again Sherman stopped, using his glasses to study the landscape. He still had seen no Confederate troops. He was still convinced this attack was only a small-scale raid.

And then, beneath the pines on the far side of the stream, sunlight glinted on bayonets. The bayonets were moving toward his left, a small river of glittering light that grew bigger and bigger. Wherever he turned his glasses there was the gleam of bayonets, hundreds upon hundreds of them.

Sherman whirled his horse and galloped to where Colonel Appler stood, white-faced and trembling. "Colonel," Sherman snapped, "you must stand your ground at all costs. You have a good battery on your right to help. I'll send reserves." Then he was gone, his staff pounding after him.

A few moments later Colonel Appler was also gone, but not to send reserves. He had taken one long look at the advancing Confederates, then a look at his own wavering line of inexperienced soldiers. Then he bawled, "Retreat! Save yourselves!"—and fled.

Some of his troops fled with him, but not all. Some rallied around their junior officers and fought as bravely that day as any men at Shiloh—and that was very bravely indeed.

In no battle in all the war was there fiercer fighting or greater courage shown by soldiers. The inexperienced Confederate columns struck along a wide front. In some places they caught the Union forces still asleep, or at breakfast, and turned parts of the battle into a wild rout. In other places they found the Yankees ready and waiting, lying in back of fallen trees, rocks, behind peach trees in the orchard, firing steadily and with deadly effect.

Sherman himself seemed to be everywhere. And whatever the fears that had tortured and driven him almost insane a few months before, they were gone now that he faced actual danger. His mind had never worked faster or more clearly. Wherever his line broke he was there, rallying the men, forming a new line to carry on the fight. When reserves were needed, he knew where to find them. With the sound of guns shaking the earth itself, he did not shout as much as he had done when there was no battle. He did not wave his arms as much when he talked. The cigar clenched in his teeth went out; only now and then did he find time to relight it.

A bullet struck Sherman's horse. It staggered and fell, throwing the general clear. Quickly he regained his feet. A member of Sherman's staff swung down from the saddle to give the general his own horse. He was a young lieutenant who a few days before had complained of a lack of action. Now he was getting more action than he had bargained for. The next moment Sherman was on the lieutenant's horse and riding again.

A buckshot, probably fired by some Confederate who was using the same shotgun with which he had hunted deer back home, ripped through the palm of Sherman's right hand. Using his left hand and his teeth, he knotted a handkerchief around it. But even now he was not looking at his hand. His eyes were studying the battlefield as if it were a map. He might have been planning the next move of toy soldiers in a game.

A bullet cut the shoulder strap of Sherman's

uniform, raising a welt on his skin. He sat with his wounded right hand inside his shirt, his left hand holding the horse's reins, motionless.

At noon a second horse was shot from under him. For a moment he watched the wounded animal paw the ground in misery. Later he would say that the sight of dead men on the battlefield did not send him into shock. But the sight of dead and dying horses somehow disturbed him deep inside. Perhaps he felt that all soldiers took a gamble with their lives but that innocent animals had nothing to do with war.

The Confederate attack kept on, wave after wave. Gradually the Confederates drove the Union forces back. Time after time Sherman reformed his lines, attacked, retreated. In one place the armies fought back and forth across a meadow until, as Sherman reported later, there were "ten thousand men lying in a field not more than a mile by half a mile." A Confederate soldier said that a man could walk across this same field "using bodies for stepping stones."

In the peach orchards bullets knocked the blossoms from the trees. They drifted down on the dead and dying men beneath them. Cannon balls ripped limbs from the trees, tore the trees themselves apart and tore the men beneath them. In other places men fought through thick underbrush, sometimes coming within a foot or two of the enemy before seeing him, fighting him then with bayonets and knives.

Gradually the Confederates pushed forward, capturing the tents where the Union forces had slept the night before. Later Sherman said, "Our wounded mingled with Rebels, charred and blackened by the burning tents and grass, crawling about begging for someone to end their misery. . . ."

It had to end. By late twilight the Union forces had been pushed back to a line between the Tennessee River on one side and a small creek on the other. Perhaps one last, fierce charge might have broken it and given the South victory. But the Southern forces were no longer able to attack. General Albert Sidney Johnston had been killed. Beauregard, now in command, knew that his men were exhausted. Many were without ammunition. Some who had not eaten all day, or even the day before, had left the fighting to search the captured Union camps for food.

And so the two armies rested, waiting for the next day.

During the night it rained hard. But the rain, even the low, rumbling thunder, could not drown out the moans and screams of wounded men lying by the thousands on the battlefield. Stretcher bearers worked in the darkness. But there were few stretcher bearers, and even fewer doctors. Most of the wounded lay where they had fallen. The rain stopped and the night turned cold. Men died in puddles of water rimmed by frosted blood. One Confederate soldier heard hogs feeding on the dead.

That night General Beauregard set up his headquarters in what had been Sherman's tent. But he already knew the battle was probably lost. He knew that General Don Carlos Buell had finally reached the Union lines, bringing an entire new

Northern army with him. General Lew Wallace had arrived with a fresh division. The Union forces now outnumbered the Confederates by two to one or more. In Sherman's old tent an uneducated but brilliant Southern general named Nathan Bedford Forrest was saying, "If the Yankees attack tomorrow, they'll whup the tar out of us."

And with daylight the Yankees attacked. Once more Sherman was everywhere. Some of the fighting on the second day at Shiloh was as fierce as anything on the first day. But the Southern troops were falling back now—not broken, not running, but fighting as they retreated. When darkness once more put an end to the fighting, Beauregard kept his men retreating. The Union army was too exhausted to follow. The Battle of Shiloh was over.

10

The Battle of Vicksburg

Not long after Shiloh, Brigadier General Sherman was made a major general. But the battle had done more for Sherman than merely win him a promotion. Shiloh marked a decided turning point in his life. He would continue to be moody, to have his ups and downs. But in the flame, death and suffering of Shiloh, he had gained a self-confidence that would never leave him. He had proved his courage at Bull Run, but what he found at Shiloh was more important. Bull Run had been a defeat; Shiloh had been a victory. More than that, the victory was, at least in part, due to Sherman himself, not only to his courage but to his leadership and knowledge. After Shiloh he would still suffer periods of depression. But they would not be as long or as intense as before.

Sherman still believed that the Mississippi River was the key to the entire war. Even before the war began he had said, "Whoever controls the Mississippi will win the war." Now he was delighted

86

when he got orders from General Grant to take part in an attack on Vicksburg, Mississippi.

In the late fall of 1862 the Union already controlled most of the great river. From Memphis north it was in federal hands. The Union navy had captured New Orleans and the southern part of the river. But between the two, the city of Vicksburg was almost impregnable. As long as it was in Southern hands, it blocked the river like a dam. But once Vicksburg fell, it would not only open the river for Northern use—it would also cut the Confederacy into two parts.

"With the Mississippi in our hands," Sherman had told Grant, "the Confederacy will be doomed. The rest of the war may take time, but the South cannot win."

Grant agreed, and together he and Sherman laid careful plans.

With the main body of the army, Grant would strike south along the railroad that led from Tennessee to Jackson, Mississippi, then east to Vicksburg. This would force General John Pemberton, who commanded the Southern forces around Vicksburg, to move his army north to stop Grant. Meanwhile Sherman, with 40,000 men, would be going downstream by boat. He would land just north of Vicksburg, catch the city by surprise with most of its defenders away, and take it by storm.

On December 19, 1862, Sherman marched his men aboard their gunboats and transports and headed downstream. On Christmas Day he was at a place called Milliken's Bend just above Vicksburg. Here the force left the Mississippi and entered the

Yazoo River, aiming for the spot where Sherman planned to launch his attack.

The weather was cold and rainy. Both the Mississippi and Yazoo were in flood and the brown, muddy waters spread out for miles. In places only the tops of fence posts, sometimes only the tops of trees or flooded barns, showed above the water.

Two days after Christmas Sherman put his men ashore on what, due to the flood, had actually become an island. But the bayou that lay between it and the high bluffs above Vicksburg was shallow and could be forded.

He had had no word from Grant since leaving Memphis. In fact there was no way for Grant to get word to him. So he could only assume that Grant was fighting his way south along the railroad and that Confederate General Pemberton had taken most of the troops out of Vicksburg to meet Grant.

Actually, Confederate cavalry had cut in back of Grant's army at a place called Holly Springs in northern Mississippi and destroyed his supplies. Grant had been forced to retreat. So Pemberton not only had the main body of his troops in Vicksburg, but he also knew about Sherman's advance —and he was ready and waiting for him.

The battle opened in the final days of December 1862 with Union artillery bombarding the bluffs on the Southern side of the bayou. Then the federal infantry advanced. Pounded by Southern rifles and artillery, they waded the bayou, drove the Confederates out of a first, small line of trenches—and came to a stop.

Beyond this line rose the bluffs. From them Southern artillery and small arms lashed the Northern soldiers. They could not fight their way up the bluffs and they could not retreat across the bayou without being in the open.

To Sherman it was soon obvious that his attack had failed. Even so, it was night before he could get his men—those who had not been killed or captured—back across the bayou and out of range of the Southern guns.

This was the first large-scale action in which Sherman was on his own. He had lost over 1,700 men, the Confederates only a hundred or so. Now he was bitter about his defeat, but still determined to use his men to good advantage while waiting for Grant.

Admiral David Dixon Porter, a tough, thick-bearded sailor, was the naval officer in charge of the boats that had brought Sherman's troops down the Mississippi. He and Sherman had quickly become friends. Now Sherman called on Porter in the cabin of his flagship.

"I've lost seventeen hundred men," he said slowly. "When the word gets back north, the newspapers and reporters will blame it all on me."

Admiral Porter shrugged. "Don't worry about newspapers, Cump. This is war. Before it's over you'll lose seventeen thousand men."

Sherman kept pacing the cabin. He was never good at sitting still. "We'll take Vicksburg yet," he said. "But only after Grant arrives with the main body of his army. Meanwhile, I want to do something to wipe out this licking."

Porter shrugged. "I'll take you anywhere there's water enough for these gunboats."

"How about Arkansas Post?"

This was a fort on the Arkansas River about 125 miles from Vicksburg. It wasn't a big fort, but left in Confederate hands it might cause trouble during the next attack on Vicksburg.

"Let's go," Porter said.

The gunboats and transports beat their slow way up the flooded Mississippi. On January 10 they were only a few miles below Arkansas Post and Sherman took his men ashore. With only light fighting they captured the fort, installed a Union garrison, then returned to Milliken's Bend. Here, on January 17, General Grant arrived to take overall command of the Vicksburg campaign.

Vicksburg lay on the east bank of the Mississippi. The combination of high bluffs, big defense guns and the river itself made any attack from the west practically impossible. To the north, where Sherman had staged his earlier attack, the country was a vast tangle of rivers, bayous and swamps. The easiest way for an army to approach Vicksburg was from the east or south. But Grant's original attempt to drive from Tennessee toward Jackson, east of Vicksburg, had been defeated. And to get south of the city from Milliken's Bend, the boats would have to run straight past the powerful guns of the fort.

Grant tried one way after another in an effort to find a water route around the north. Sherman and Admiral Porter were involved in one of these efforts in which Porter took five gunboats to search out a possible water route around the city. Sherman and an infantry unit went along to help.

It was a nasty job. Trees hung over the narrow, twisting streams and limbs had to be chopped off before the boats could pass. Snakes, raccoons, possums and birds' nests fell out of the trees onto the decks of the gunboats. Confederate soldiers, ranging ahead of the boats, cut down other trees to block the way. But, heavily armed, the gunboats were usually able to batter their way past obstructions that had to be cleared before the wooden barges carrying the infantry could follow. As a result, at some points there might be miles between the gunboats and the barges.

At last the gunboats reached a point where they could go no farther. And now, suddenly, the Confederates began to cut down trees behind them, blocking their retreat. From the swamps Confederate snipers started picking off the sailors working on deck. All at once it looked very much as if Confederate infantry was going to capture five federal gunboats.

At this time Sherman's men were about twenty miles behind, where they had stopped to clear a bayou of fallen trees. Across the water Sherman could hear the distant booming of guns. But he felt sure the gunboats could defend themselves and kept his men working where they were.

That night Sherman was asleep when an orderly awakened him. "A messenger from Admiral Porter, sir."

The messenger was a Negro. Wet, muddy from head to toe, shivering with cold, he stepped forward and took a piece of chewing tobacco from his pocket. Rolled inside the tobacco was a note from Porter. The Admiral needed help—and fast.

Sherman looked at the Negro messenger. Yesterday this man had been a slave. Tonight he had risked his life for white men who represented liberty. Why? Sherman had lived in the South; he had been inclined to agree with the Southern claim that most Negroes were happy and content to be slaves. But was it really true?

There was no time to think about it now. "Give this man dry clothes," he told the orderly. "Food, and something to drink." Then he was pulling on his coat, calling for messengers, giving orders. With his men crowded on barges pulled by tugs, Sherman set out to follow Porter.

The night was pitch dark. Trees slammed against the tug. The pilothouse was carried away. Then the smokestack. Before they had gone three miles the way was totally blocked.

Sherman led his men over the side of the barge into waist-deep water. Men held their guns and ammunition overhead to keep them dry. Some carried candles. The pale flames gave almost no light to the soldiers who carried them, but they helped keep the troops together—a host of flickering fireflies moving slowly between the muddy waters and the black overhanging trees. Men slipped and fell and their candles went out, and they lit them again from those of their comrades. Far ahead, Sherman could hear the steady booming of cannon.

Daylight came cold and gray. Sherman kept

moving ahead, sometimes in water, sometimes in mud, stumbling with weariness but still going. The sun rose higher and the sound of the firing grew closer.

About noon Sherman suddenly came out of the swamp into a cotton field. On the far side of the field he could see the tops of the gunboats and the flash of their guns. Confederate rifles answered from nearby trees.

With a great shout the Union infantry surged across the cotton field. There was the sharp, brittle clatter of rifle fire. And suddenly it was all over. There had been only a few Confederates. As Sherman's troops rushed forward, the Southerners moved back into the swamp. Quickly the sailors on the gunboats chopped apart the trees blocking their retreat. Still there was no room to turn the boats around. They had to back, slowly, with the infantry patrolling alongside. Finally they could turn. The soldiers came aboard and the whole force made its way back to the Mississippi and Milliken's Bend.

But the City of Vicksburg was still in Southern hands, and General Grant, pacing slowly back and forth chewing on his cigar, had to find some way to capture it.

It was April 1863 before he finally made up his mind. He would march his army south down the west bank of the Mississippi, he said. The guns of Vicksburg could not reach them there.

"But how," Sherman asked him, "are they going to cross back over to reach Vicksburg? And what about supplies?"

"That depends on Admiral Porter. If he can run his gunboats past the Vicksburg batteries, we can meet them thirty miles or so downstream, cross over in them, and hit Vicksburg from the other side."

Sherman didn't like the idea. He didn't believe the gunboats could move directly past the Vicksburg batteries and survive. But Admiral Porter laughed. "We'll try. I'd rather face the batteries than those swamps again."

The dash would be made on the night of April 16. Early that same day Sherman, with a small detachment, marched south along the west bank of the river. Just below Vicksburg and out of reach of its guns, he assembled a few rowboats. After darkness the boats rowed out to try to pick up any survivors from ships sunk as they passed the city.

For awhile there was only the sound of the river. Then, abruptly, came the boom of a gun, followed almost instantly by the monstrous, rolling thunder of cannon upon cannon. The gunboats had been spotted by the Confederates. Shore batteries were firing, the gunboats hurling their shells back in return.

The night sky began to turn faintly pink, orange, then red. The Confederates had set fire to abandoned houses along both banks of the stream and now the gunboats were outlined against the flames. Cannon balls threw up great geysers of water, glittering and vanishing against the firelight.

The gunboats were battered, but only one was sunk. The others came through. Yet even now Sherman had no faith in Grant's plan. He didn't like the idea of an entire army being led through the heart of enemy country with no base of supplies and no supply line. "How," he asked Grant, "are you going to feed the men?"

Grant chewed on his unlit cigar. "I thought we'd live off the country," he said. "Braxton Bragg did it when he led his Rebels up into Kentucky. I think we can do it in Mississippi."

Sherman disagreed. But he was totally loyal to Grant, and if Grant ordered him to march through the heart of Mississippi without a supply line, he would march.

So it was that the Union army marched southward along the west bank of the Mississippi for some fifty miles below Vicksburg, crossed over in Porter's boats and turned north again.

Over the dusty Mississippi roads the federal soldiers moved rapidly. Every morning small parties of soldiers left the main body and raided the countryside for food. From nearby farms they took cattle and pigs, chickens and ducks and turkeys, better food than any supply train could have furnished.

Sherman watched in amazement. His men were lean, tough and healthy. They were marching miles every day, singing, laughing, sure of themselves. And very soon Sherman, too, was sure of them. The Confederates had no army in Mississippi that could stop them.

One night he was asleep in a cabin beside the road when an orderly awoke him. "General Grant just rode up, sir."

Sherman had not seen Grant in person since they moved south from Vicksburg. Now he jumped up, pulled on his trousers, and quickly ran outside.

There were half a dozen mounted officers in the yard. Soldiers held burning torches. By their light, Sherman saw Grant swing down from his horse. Sherman ran up to him. "I want to congratulate you, General, on the success of your plan. It's working!" There was no envy, only real admiration in his voice. "And it is your plan too, General, nobody's but yours. Because none of the rest of us believed in it!"

Grant nodded, a little shyly. For a long moment the two men stood looking at each other by the light of the flaming torches. Perhaps they were both remembering another time they had met—on a street in St. Louis when they were both without money, jobs or hope.

In Vicksburg, General Pemberton was trying desperately to decide what to do next. He no longer knew just where the Union army was. When he sent soldiers to cut its supply line, there wasn't any supply line to be found, just a long trail of burned barns and looted farms.

It wasn't until the Union army neared Vicksburg that Pemberton brought his forces out to meet them. There were several brief skirmishes and the outmanned Southerners were driven back into the city. Then for two days Grant brought up his cannon and men, preparing for one final furious attack that would end the campaign.

There was no river on this side of Vicksburg, but there were high bluffs, very much like those that had stopped Sherman's first attack several months before. In places the bluffs were cut by deep gullies. But these gullies came to blind ends. And while Pemberton had been worrying, uncertain what to do next, he had also been building fortifications.

Early on the morning of May 22, 1863, Grant's massed artillery opened fire. It hurled shells at the high bluffs where the Confederates were dug in. It pounded the trenches. And then, at 10 A.M., Grant sent his infantry forward.

One company, moving steadily up a brush-grown ravine, came suddenly into the open with Confederates looking down on it from high bluffs on three sides. There was an appalling, deafening roar of Confederate guns. In a single volley every man in the lead Union company was killed or wounded, except two. Other companies came on, to be cut to pieces or driven back.

In some places the Union soldiers reached the foot of the cliffs, so close that the Southern cannon could not fire down upon them. The Rebel artillerymen simply lit fuses on their cannon balls and rolled them down the cliff to explode among the federal infantry.

The attack was obviously hopeless. Grant was about to call it off when one of his generals, John McClernand, sent word that his troops had broken into the Southern lines. If Sherman's men could make a little more effort, McClernand said, the entire force might break through into Vicksburg.

Sherman was standing beside Grant when the message arrived. Neither really believed it. They both knew that McClernand was brave, reckless even, and also given to unrealistic bragging. But in the heat of battle there was no time to check. If there was a chance to win by continuing the fight, it had to be done now. "We'll attack again," said Sherman.

Once more his men charged the high bluffs and went down the narrow ravines. Once more the Southern guns cut them to pieces and drove them back. By now it was obvious that McClernand's men had never broken the Southern lines at all, and Grant called off the attack. In a few hours he had lost three thousand men and gained nothing.

Now the two armies stood facing one another. Grant could not break through the Southern defenses to capture Vicksburg, but neither could Pemberton's outnumbered men break free. Union gunboats patrolled the river on the west. To the east, Grant's army lay in a great semicircle. No food could get to the people in the city, and no supplies. Day by day they grew leaner, hungrier, more ragged. Confederate soldiers ate their mules, their horses. People in the city ate dogs and cats.

The siege continued through the rest of May . . . through all of June. On the Fourth of July, 1863, General Pemberton raised the white flag, and the city of Vicksburg surrendered.

One of the Confederate prisoners taken at

Vicksburg was Captain David Boyd—the same Dave Boyd who had been Sherman's closest friend at the Louisiana Military Academy. When Sherman heard he was among the prisoners, he had Boyd brought to his tent. For a moment the two men stared at each other. Then, half laughing, half crying, they began to pound each other on the back. It was about this time that Admiral David Porter came in. He watched the two men hugging each other. "Cump," he said, "who's your Southern friend?"

Still laughing, Sherman said, "He thinks he's a captain in the Confederate army. Actually, he's just my old friend and professor from the Louisiana State Seminary of Learning and Military Academy."

The tears in Boyd's eyes were not from laughter now. "Cump," he asked, "do you remember the school motto? It was cut in marble over the door."

"I do," Sherman said. "I quoted it in my letter of resignation to the Governor: 'The Union—*esto perpetua*.' The Union—forever."

Boyd nodded. "Only it's not there any more. They've had it chiseled out, cut away. That shows how things have changed."

"Maybe," Sherman said slowly, "maybe, someday, the people of the South will want to put it back, and keep it there: The Union—forever."

Boyd was as starved and ragged as the other Confederates at Vicksburg. Sherman had him fed and given new clothes. He arranged to have his friend paroled and sent home.

Then he turned once more toward the war.

99

11

Vicksburg to Chattanooga

With the Confederacy split in half, Sherman for the first time felt sure the end of the war was near. Since the South no longer had any real chance of military victory, he thought, the Confederate leaders could now surrender with honor.

Sherman wanted to make that end as easy and honorable as possible. He sent food and medicine to the Confederate hospitals. From army supplies he furnished food for the hungry women and children in Vicksburg. He ordered his soldiers to stop stealing from Southern homes and farms. The truth is that his men paid little attention to the order, but Sherman tried to enforce it. He wrote to Grant: "The amount of plundering and stealing done by our army makes me ashamed of it. . . . I have endeavored to repress this class of crime, but you know how difficult it is to fix the guilt among the great mass of the army."

The fighting temporarily suspended, Sherman's family came down to visit him. His son

Willie was nine years old now, and Cump's favorite child. Willie loved to play at being one of his father's soldiers, and the soldiers themselves quickly adopted him. They tailored him a uniform from scraps of their own, made him a small gun, let him drill with them and called him "Sergeant Willie." Proudly Sherman took Willie with him as he rode about the camp and sometimes let his son stand beside him during inspections.

So in a kind of peaceful lull Sherman passed the end of July, all of August and part of September 1863.

Judged in the light of history, he was right in believing that the South no longer had a chance of winning a military victory. Some Southern leaders understood this as well as he did. But the South still did have one chance to win—not a military victory, but a political one.

In the North many people had long since grown weary of the fighting. Many of them were now willing to let the Union be divided if only it would put an end to the war. On the other hand, President Lincoln was determined to save the Union at all costs. However, there was to be a Presidential election in the fall of 1864, and it was likely that the man who ran against Lincoln might want peace at any price. The outcome of the election would depend on how the war went in the meantime.

And in September 1863 it was going very badly for the Union. At the Battle of Chickamauga, just south of Chattanooga, Tennessee, a Union army under General William Rosecrans was defeated and driven back against the city. Here it found itself in a situation somewhat like that of the Confederate army in Vicksburg. It could defend itself against attack; but behind it lay wild, mountainous country through which it would be almost impossible to retreat. In front of it, holding a high ridge that seemed impossible to attack, stood the Confederate army of General Braxton Bragg.

However, at Vicksburg the South had had no other army in the area it could use to raise the siege. The Union had vast reserves of men and supplies, and quickly General Hooker was ordered to go to Chattanooga with part of the Army of the Potomac. General Grant, then in New Orleans, came to Chattanooga to take overall command. Sherman was ordered to bring his Army of the Tennessee from Vicksburg to Chattanooga.

Sherman began the move by boat, carrying his troops up the Mississippi to Memphis. His family went with him, Willie Sherman as excited as if he were actually going into battle with his father. But the upriver trip had barely started when the child complained of a headache. When General Sherman put his hand on the boy's forehead, he found it was burning hot.

An army doctor was called. He examined the boy, then turned slowly to face his parents. "He has typhoid fever," he said.

There was little anyone could do. At Memphis the child was taken ashore. Other doctors were called in. But within 24 hours Willie was dead.

Sherman was heartbroken. "Of all my children," he said, "Willie seemed the most precious." He wrote a letter to his soldiers, thanking them for their kindness to the child, saying, "Willie was, or thought he was, a sergeant. . . . I have seen his eyes brighten and heard his heart beat as he beheld the battalion under arms and asked me if they were not *real* soldiers. Child as he was, he had the enthusiasm . . . and love of country which should animate all soldiers."

And because Sherman himself was a soldier, he could not put aside his job because of his grief. A military detail was assigned to accompany Mrs. Sherman and Willie's body to Lancaster for burial. With the Army of the Tennessee, Sherman marched eastward toward Chattanooga.

It was November when he arrived. He found Grant and the rest of the Union forces waiting, the battle plan already formed.

Grant's forces far outnumbered the Confederates. But the Confederates were located atop a long, high bluff called Missionary Ridge. The ridge rose steeply some 500 feet above a wide, level plain south of Chattanooga. Heavily fortified, the ridge itself seemed impossible to take by frontal attack.

Grant's plan was to send General Hooker against one end of the ridge, Sherman against the other. The Army of the Cumberland, under General George Thomas, would drive against the middle. But this frontal assault was not supposed to be anything except a feint. It was intended to keep Bragg from sending reserves to help the men on the flanks. The main attacks, by Sherman and Hooker, were to drive down the ridge from each end and crush the Confederates between them.

It was hoped that Sherman's attack would be

a surprise. His men circled far behind Grant's lines, then swung back to the Tennessee River. Sherman already had 116 crude, small boats prepared. At midnight he sent a few of them, loaded with troops, across the river. There were only a few Confederate pickets here and the federal scouts easily drove them back. Then the rest of the boats swung out on the river, Sherman himself in one of the first. The boats were lined up, planks laid across them to form a bridge and the troops marched over.

With the first daylight Sherman's troops hit the end of Missionary Ridge. There was fog and a drizzling rain. The men could see only a few yards ahead of them. The Confederates in their rifle pits and shallow trenches could not see the attackers until the blue uniforms loomed out of the mist only a few yards away. There were short, sharp flashes of gunfire, brief hand-to-hand encounters with bayonets. The Yankee troops drove the Rebels up the slope far more easily than had been expected.

Then the rain stopped and the sun burned the fog away. Sherman, moving ahead with his troops, learned suddenly that his maps had been wrong and he wasn't where he thought he was.

The maps had shown Missionary Ridge as one

long continuous ridge. Actually this end of the ridge was broken into a number of steep hills. Sherman's men had taken the first hill—the main part of the ridge still lay ahead. When Sherman's men moved toward it through bright morning sunlight Confederate fire poured down upon them. The leading wave was cut to pieces and driven back. Other men took their places to be smashed back. And others followed them with the same result.

At the other end of the ridge things went no better for the Union forces. Hooker's men had captured the slope of Lookout Mountain, but when they turned from there toward Missionary Ridge itself the lead column got its directions mixed and wandered away. The men who did attack the ridge were beaten back.

General George Thomas, who commanded the Army of the Cumberland, holding the Union center, had been Cump Sherman's best friend at West Point. Now, as the sun rose higher and the roar of Sherman's guns grew louder, Thomas stood with General Grant on a little hill called Orchard Knob. From here they could see the wide, level plain where the Army of the Cumberland waited, and beyond that, rising sharply against the autumn sky, Missionary Ridge.

By afternoon it became obvious that Sherman's men were making no progress. Grant sent Sherman orders, "Attack again."

Sherman stared at the sheet of paper. Surely Grant could not know his men were being cut down.

"Signal Grant," Sherman told an orderly. "Make sure this is the proper order."

From the crest of the hill the signal flags wig-wagged back and forth. From Orchard Knob flags sent back Grant's order: "Attack again."

One of Sherman's officers was his foster-brother, Hugh Ewing. "Hugh," Sherman told him "take your division and hit the extreme left. Keep your men in formation until you reach the hill."

"And after that?"

"Take the hill—if you can." He reached out and touched Hugh's arm. "Don't call for help unless you really need it."

So the men in blue went forward again—with no more luck than before.

On Orchard Knob, Grant turned to Thomas. "I think it's time you sent your men in. They should be able to take the first line of trenches at the foot of the ridge."

Except for a heavy beard, Thomas looked much as he had at West Point—stout, solid, slow. His mind worked in the same slow, methodical way. He was always cautious, careful, without fear, but he didn't like to sacrifice his men and he didn't believe anybody could capture that long, fortified bluff, maybe not even the trenches at its foot. So he stood there, combing his beard with his fingers, and not even Grant could hurry him.

Finally he gave the word. What followed was one of the miracles of the war.

Many of Thomas' men had been in the Battle of Chickamauga where they were badly beaten by the Confederates. They had been bitter about this defeat ever since. Now in the late afternoon came the order to attack, and with a roar they went forward—18,000 men, four army divisions spread in a solid line two miles long across a plain so level and empty it was like a stage.

The front of the solid blue mass hit the Confederate trenches at the foot of the ridge and engulfed it. Then there was a pause, a brief pause, with the mass of blue-clad men still coming across the plain, seemingly without end. There was no order for the soldiers to climb the ridge; nobody thought they could. But with a wild shout they started up it, poured up it like some giant wave crashing against a cliff and rising, leaping up, ever upward.

The Confederates who held Missionary Ridge were veteran troops. They were the same who had smashed Rosecrans' army at Chickamauga. They were veterans, but some were old men, and some were no more than boys. They were mostly ragged, poorly fed. And suddenly, at the sight of the blue mass rushing toward them like a tide that could not be stopped, they turned and ran.

The battle of Chattanooga was over.

Next day a Union officer climbed Missionary Ridge. Most of the men who had died there were still unburied and the officer stood looking down at the body of a Confederate soldier. "He was," the officer wrote, "not over fifteen years of age, and very slender in size. He was clothed in a cotton suit and was barefooted—barefooted on that cold and wet 24th day of November. I examined his haversack. For a day's ration there were a handful of black beans, a few pieces of sorghum, and a half-dozen roasted acorns."

12

The Fall of Atlanta

After the battle of Missionary Ridge there was a brief lull in the fighting. Sherman took a few days' leave in which to visit his family and stand with bowed head beside the grave of his son Willie. Then he rejoined the army.

Soon afterward President Lincoln made changes in the high command of the federal armies. U. S. Grant, who had commanded in the west, was now to command all the Union armies, east and west. Sherman in turn was given Grant's old job as commander of the western armies. Grant was about to leave for Washington, but first he and Sherman met in a Cincinnati hotel to make plans.

"I had hoped the war would be over by now," Sherman said. "Ever since Vicksburg fell, the Confederacy has been split in two. The South can't win. But their newspapers and politicians keep right on ranting, and sending boys out to be killed."

Grant chewed on an unlit cigar. "I expect Jeff Davis is hoping Lincoln won't be reelected and that

108

the new President, whoever he is, will simply let the South go."

Sherman began to pace back and forth across the room. His uniform was rumpled from the long train ride to Cincinnati, his red hair as uncombed as ever, and there were flecks of gray now in his short-cropped beard. The last two years had carved deep lines into the face of the 44-year-old general that gave him a hawklike look. "The people in the North will never let the Union be destroyed."

"I hope not," Grant said. "And we've still got eight months before the election." He stood up, moving in his short-legged, awkward way to a table where a map was spread. "Let's get to work."

The plan they fixed upon was simple enough. The Confederacy had two main armies: one, under General Robert E. Lee, was stationed in front of Richmond, Virginia; the other, under Joseph E. Johnston, was quartered at Dalton, in northern Georgia. Summarizing the Union strategy, Grant said that he would take personal command of the Army of the Potomac and go after General Lee. He would force Lee to fight, and keep fighting, until Lee's army wore out. At the same time, Sherman would take the western armies and go after General Johnston. But he would not only destroy Johnston's army: he would try to hit at the South's economic strength, its ability to keep fighting.

"And the South's economic strength, what there is left of it, is centered in Atlanta," Sherman said.

Grant nodded. "But I don't want to tell you exactly where to go. You'll be governed by circumstances. And you'll be on your own."

The thought no longer frightened Cump Sherman. Fully confident, he went back to his headquarters in Tennessee, called his senior officers and began to lay plans for his own campaign.

Under his command Sherman now had a force of approximately 100,000 men divided into three armies. There was the Army of the Cumberland under General Thomas, the Army of the Ohio under General John Schofield and the Army of the Tennessee under General James McPherson.

Confronting them, General Johnston had approximately 60,000 Confederates gathered in front of Dalton. But Joseph Johnston was one of the smartest military men in the South, and Sherman knew it. Not for a moment did he underestimate his foe. Trapping Johnston's army wouldn't be easy. And if Sherman made a serious mistake, Johnston might catch the Union armies scattered and smash them in units.

In early May 1864, Sherman began his move. From Chattanooga, where he had his headquarters, a railroad led to Dalton, Georgia, about 25 miles away. A little to the east of Chattanooga was another railroad that also led to Dalton. Sherman sent Thomas and the Army of the Cumberland straight down one of these railroads, Schofield and the Army of the Ohio down the other. Without much trouble, they drove back a thin line of Confederate pickets. Just north of Dalton, Thomas and Schofield joined forces and halted, faced by Johnston's dug-in and fortified main line of defense.

Sherman had suspected all along that a frontal attack against these defenses would produce terrible casualties, with victory uncertain. Consequently he had sent McPherson and the Army of the Tennessee —24,000 men—on a long sweep to the south and along the right of Thomas and Schofield. This Army of the Tennessee was Sherman's old command. These were the men he had trained himself; the ones in whom he had the most faith. They were veterans—tough, lean, able to endure long, swift marches under almost any conditions.

Now he meant them to circle back of a range of low mountains, slip through narrow gaps in the hills without being seen and cut the railroad supplying Johnston's army near a town called Resaca. At this point, Thomas and Schofield would smash into the Confederates from the north. McPherson would attack from the south, and Johnston's army would be destroyed between them.

It was shrewd strategy, and it almost worked. While McPherson circled to the southwest, Thomas and Schofield launched small but fierce attacks on the main defense line. These were beaten back. The Union losses were heavy, but the attacks kept Johnston's attention centered on the armies ahead of him. Meanwhile McPherson and the Army of the Tennessee passed through the mountain gaps and reached a point only two miles from Resaca. McPherson sent Sherman a message saying, "I propose to cut the railroad, if possible, then fall back and take a strong position near the gorge."

Sherman was eating supper when the message came. He hit the camp table with his fist so hard the dishes bounced. "I've got Joe Johnston dead!" he shouted. "Now we'll ride and tell Thomas to strike!"

But before Sherman, riding himself through the night, could reach General Thomas, another messenger overtook him.

Things had gone wrong at Resaca. McPherson had 24,000 men when he broke out of the mountains, and between him and the railroad were less than 2,000 Confederates. But McPherson had not known this. His skirmish line, moving slowly forward, met furious resistance and halted. Darkness fell and they had not yet reached the railroad. McPherson, overestimating the force in front of him, called his men back and sent Sherman word that he had not cut the line.

Sherman knew immediately that the whole plan had failed. Now that Johnston was warned, he would have reinforcements opposite McPherson before the Army of the Tennessee could strike again.

Sherman wasted no time on anger. New plans had to be made and he rode on to talk with Thomas and Schofield. All night and next day plans were drawn. Then, leaving only a small, well-fortified force in front of Johnston's main position, Sherman sent his whole army circling toward Resaca.

For two days and nights he had worked almost without sleep and with little food. About ten o'clock in the morning he turned his horse off the road, lay down under a tree and went to sleep.

Troops were marching past steadily. One of them blinked when he saw the man with the stars on his shoulders stretched out on the ground. "Ain't that a general?" he asked.

One of Sherman's orderlies answered him, "It's Uncle Billy Sherman."

"Well," the soldier said, "this is some way to run a army. The commanding general is drunk and passed out at ten in the morning."

Instantly Sherman sat up. "You!" he called. "I'm not drunk. While you were sleeping, I was working all night. Now I'm trying to take a nap."

The soldier, red-faced, marched on while his friends howled with laughter. "Uncle Billy," they said, "sleeps with one eye and one ear open."

When Sherman and his main force joined McPherson opposite Resaca, they found Johnston waiting for them. He had retreated from Dalton, bringing his men down the railroad, destroying it behind him, and had set up new defenses. Once more Sherman sent units to pound the Confederate lines, trying to find a weak spot. Once more they were driven back. And once more Sherman used his numerical advantage to send men circling southwest in an effort to get behind Johnston. And once more Johnston retreated, holding his army together, destroying what was left of the railroad as he went.

It was the start of a campaign that became almost as formal as a dance, a kind of gigantic waltz performed by 160,000 men who moved to the music conducted by two excellent generals. Johnston would retreat and halt where the hills or a river gave his small army a natural line of defense. Sherman would move forward, strike Johnston's defense line, find he could not break it, then move part of his army in a half circle, trying to get at Johnston from behind.

In doing this there was always the danger that the Confederates might catch the Union army divided and smash it. But Sherman had traveled over much of this country years before as a young lieutenant. He still remembered it and used that knowledge well. Also, whenever his army halted, Sherman had his men build defense works so strong that one part of the force could safely hold its ground while another part circled.

Sherman could never catch Johnston in a trap. But Johnston, with the smaller army, could never hold Sherman in one place. Slowly, halting and starting to the awful music of cannon, the two armies moved southeast, closer and closer to Atlanta.

Johnston had one advantage. As he retreated his supply lines grew shorter while those of Sherman grew longer. As the Confederates retreated they tore up the railroad that led back to Sherman's base in Tennessee. In turn, Sherman's engineers repaired it almost as fast as the Confederates destroyed it. Often the Southerners could hear the whistle of Union engines moving over track they had wrecked only the day before.

Only once did Sherman alter his tactics. In late June, Johnston took up a position in the Kenesaw Mountain country. It was one of the strongest natural positions he had held. Perhaps this was one reason Sherman chose this place to make a straight frontal attack. He may have thought that Johnston would put so much faith in the natural defenses the area offered that few soldiers would be left to defend it while the main body of the Confederate army would be shifted to meet Sherman's usual encircling movement.

Whatever his reason, Sherman sent Thomas'

army charging straight against the Confederate defenses—and lost 2,500 men. It was lesson enough for him. He called off the frontal attack and once more tried to strike at Johnston from the rear. Once again Johnston retreated. But this time when he stopped Atlanta was close behind him and there could be no further retreat.

Atlanta was the economic heart of the South. Here was one of the last of the ammunition factories in the Confederacy, along with cotton gins and ironworks. Most of the railroad lines that remained in Southern hands passed through Atlanta. The fall of Atlanta would be as serious a blow to the South as the fall of Vicksburg had been, and everybody knew it.

In his retreat from Dalton, General Joseph Johnston had proved himself a great defensive strategist. His outnumbered army had inflicted more casualties than it had suffered. It had been forced to retreat, but it had not been broken. It was still intact, still a fighting unit.

This, however, was not enough for President Jefferson Davis who had never cared much for Johnston. He wanted Sherman driven out of Georgia, and Johnston had not been able to do it. Davis removed Johnston from command and replaced him with General John B. Hood. Hood, Davis said, was a "fighting general."

He was all of that. He had been shot through the arm at Gettysburg and had lost a leg at Chickamauga. He was not a careful, cool tactician like Johnston, but a headlong battler. Now he picked what he hoped was a weak point in Sherman's lines,

115

sent his men charging to the attack—and was beaten back with heavy losses.

The Union lines edged closer and closer to Atlanta. Decatur, five miles to the east, was captured. Sherman's big guns hurled shells into Atlanta itself. They were aimed at the warehouses, railroad yards and ironworks. But there were times when they hit private homes. Fires lighted the night sky.

Hood picked another spot in the Union lines and struck with everything he could put into the fight. The attack was so sudden and so fierce that General James McPherson, in command of the Army of the Tennessee, was caught and killed by the advancing skirmish line. Sherman's own headquarters was hit by artillery fire before he could realize the seriousness of the situation. For a time the fate of Atlanta, and with it perhaps the fate of the Union, hung in the balance.

With the crash of shells around his headquarters, Sherman became a man inspired. Later one of his officers would say, "His mind seemed never so clear; his confidence never so strong; his spirit never so inspiring." With the battle whirling madly around him, Sherman took command of his own artillery. He galloped alongside the plunging horses, ordered where the guns should be swung into place, directed their fire to sweep the flank of the charging Confederate line.

And the gray attack wavered, broke and fell back. There were simply not enough Confederates to break the Union lines. Hood's men suffered almost 10,000 casualties, killed, wounded and captured. And when the day ended, they were back within their own defenses, the Union lines so close the soldiers could shout back and forth to one another.

It was after this fight that one of Sherman's men called out, "How many men you Johnny Rebs got left over there?"

And from the Confederate trenches a voice answered, "Oh, about enough for another killing."

And yet, because wars are political as well as military, the Union itself had never been so close to defeat. Sherman's army was within sight of Atlanta, yet now its progress could be measured by yards rather than miles. To people in the North, reading their newspapers, the army seemed to be making no progress at all. In the east, Grant's army was battering day after day against Lee's men in front of Richmond. The casualties were appalling.

Every day newspapers throughout the country carried long lists of the dead and wounded. More and more people were asking, "Is the Union worth it? Wouldn't it be better simply to stop the war and let the South go?"

Abraham Lincoln wanted to save the Union no matter the cost. The opposition Democratic Party wanted peace, even if it meant the destruction of the Union. In late August, with slightly more than two months left before the election, it seemed almost certain the Democrats would win. Lincoln himself wrote, "It seems exceedingly probable this administration will not be reelected."

About the same time a Southern general wrote that, according to what his spies told him, Lincoln was sure to be defeated and peace declared, "provided always that we continue to hold our own against the Yankee armies."

If the South could hold. That was it.

In front of Atlanta, Sherman once more tried his old wheeling tactic. Leaving only a few men to make a big noise and sound like a strong force, he marched the main body of his army westward, around the city, then south and east again. The move caught Hood almost completely by surprise. Sherman's army slashed across the railroad lines south of Atlanta, destroying them for miles.

When Hood finally did learn Sherman's location, it was too late. Hood's army wasn't strong enough to come out of Atlanta and drive Sherman away from the railroads. But if he stayed in Atlanta, now that the rail lines were cut, his men would starve without supplies.

There was only one thing to do. He abandoned the city. He managed to break through the light forces Sherman had left behind and got most of his men away. But they were only a fragment of an army now, ragged and hungry. They would never again play a major part in the fighting.

Without opposition, Sherman's men occupied the battered and half-burned city of Atlanta. On September 3, 1864, he sent a telegram to Lincoln: "Atlanta is ours, and fairly won!"

The news swept across the North. Atlanta had fallen! Men stood in the streets and cheered. Many who the day before had planned to vote against Lincoln instantly changed their minds.

Sherman had captured Atlanta. Now Lincoln was certain to be reelected, and the Union preserved.

13

Sherman's March to the Sea

In November 1864, about two months after the fall of Atlanta, Abraham Lincoln was overwhelmingly reelected President. And once more it seemed to Sherman that here was a time when the South could, and should, surrender with honor. Why keep sending young men to be blinded and maimed and killed when there was no longer any chance for either military or political victory?

But the Southern politicians and newspapers called on the people to keep fighting. Somehow, they said, Sherman's army would be destroyed. Somehow (there was no way to explain how) the South would win, if only the people continued to fight and suffer and die.

In Atlanta, where he had rested and resupplied his army after the capture of the city, Sherman talked it over with his friend, General Thomas. "It is always the politicians and the newspaper writers who cause wars," he said. "But it is the people who pay the price. . . . If the South wants war, there is

119

only one way for us to end it. We must destroy not only the South's ability to fight, but its will to fight. We must make war so horrible that nobody wants it."

"Your bark is worse than your bite," Thomas told him. He knew that Sherman often said things that were far more violent and bitter than he truly meant. But he also knew that, ever since Vicksburg, Sherman had been slowly developing a new attitude toward the South and the war. He still wanted the South brought back into the Union as soon and with as little suffering as possible. But he had become convinced the South would carry on the war just as long as it possibly could. He felt sure that the only way to end the war was, just as he had said, to destroy not only the ability but the will to fight.

To this end Sherman had already formed a plan.

He wanted to send Generals Thomas and Schofield, with about half the army, back to Tennessee. From there they could block any northward raids that Hood, with the small force left to him, might attempt. At the same time Sherman, with about 60,000 men, would march southeast through the very heart of Georgia until he reached the sea. There he would turn north, through the Carolinas to Virginia, toward the rear of Lee's army at Richmond.

The fall of Vicksburg had cut the South in two. The march that Sherman proposed would rip it into tatters. It would do more than that. Sherman wired Grant that such a march would show "the world, foreign and domestic, that we have a power Davis cannot resist." It might not be war, Sherman said, as much as a way to end war.

120

Grant, who was with his army near Richmond, was slow to agree. He reminded Sherman that on such a march his army would not only be moving through the heart of enemy country; it would be totally cut off from any communication with the North. And what, Grant asked, would Sherman do about supplies? Sherman reminded Grant of his own march through Mississippi to strike at Vicksburg from the rear. Then the Union army had lived off the land, and lived well. It could do it again.

Finally Grant gave his permission. In mid-November, William Tecumseh Sherman set out on a campaign that was like no other in history.

First, Atlanta was destroyed. The city had been fairly well battered by Union guns before its fall. The Confederate army had tried to burn all the supplies that it had been forced to leave behind. Now Sherman ordered all the people living in Atlanta to leave. They could go where they wished, but they had to leave. Then parties of soldiers set fire to, or blew up, everything that might be of use to the Confederacy as a fighting force: mills, warehouses, factories, railroad yards.

Private homes, churches and public buildings were not to be harmed. Sherman himself gave strict orders against this. But a wind was blowing, and flames spread. Some of the soldiers found it fun to set fires. When the vanguard of Sherman's army was 15 miles from the city it could look back and see a great, towering mass of smoke. When night came, the sky was bronze-colored with the light of fires. By the time the last federal troops left Atlanta, the city was largely a mass of ashes.

121

The army marched in four columns along four different parallel roads, making a path about sixty miles wide. No Confederate army existed within a hundred miles that could put up even a token fight, so there was little need for a scouting line of cavalry. Instead, each morning a picked group of men from each brigade took a wagon and went ahead of, or off to the sides of, the marching columns. At neighboring farms they loaded their wagons with food. They drove off any pigs and cows they might need for food, took any horses or mules they might need to ride. Then they rejoined their brigades, the wagons only half visible under the foodstuffs heaped over them.

That was the way it started, with at least a show of military discipline. Sherman's own orders had been specific, with a touch of Robin Hood about them: "As for horses, mules, wagons, etc.," he said, "they should be taken from the rich and not from the poor. Enough grain should be left for the planting of spring crops." Also: "To army corps commanders alone is entrusted the power to destroy mills, houses, cotton gins, etc., and for them this general principle is laid down. . . where the army is unmolested, no destruction of such property should be permitted, but should guerrillas or bush-whackers molest our march, or should the inhabitants burn bridges, obstruct roads, or otherwise manifest local hostility, then army commanders should order and enforce a devastation more or less relentless, according to the measure of such hostility."

The order reflected some of the personal problems troubling Sherman at this time. He was essentially a kind man, even a sentimental one. It hurt him to think of some individual family without food or shelter. Yet he was more and more coming to see himself as a kind of avenging angel, a man chosen by destiny to make the war so terrible that everyone in the South would want it to end swiftly.

Not all the officers and men of his army were as troubled by conscience. As time went on, some men foraged not only for food and supplies; they began to loot and steal for personal profit. Some began to destroy property for the sheer, childish pleasure of destruction, and sometimes to vent bitterness and anger upon the Southern population.

It was lovely country the army was crossing. There were rolling, red-clay hills and many large plantation homes with tall columns and wide porches. The autumn harvest had just been gathered. Smokehouses and barns bulged with food that was not only intended to last the winter but was also to furnish grain for the spring planting. But some foragers could not have cared less. They loaded

their wagons and set fire to the barns and smokehouses.

Along with the foragers sent out by the army
there were men called bummers. Some of these were
soldiers who, because there was little discipline on
the march, had temporarily deserted their units to
make a business of foraging for profit. Some of them
were civilians, a kind of human scum (and some
of these were Southerners as well as Yankees), who
simply took advantage of the situation.

These were the men who not only burned
barns; they forced their way into homes, stole silver
and money, took priceless china and glassware and
tossed it into wagons where it was smashed before
they had gone half a mile. They loaded their wagons
with priceless furniture from plantation homes and
tossed it into the nearest creek when the wagons
became overloaded.

At an easy 15 miles a day the army moved
southeast across Georgia. A Southern family, seeing
foragers clatter into the yard on horseback, never
knew whether they would be treated politely, and
even given supplies sometimes in case of need, or
have their home burned around them.

Eight days after leaving Atlanta, the army
reached Milledgeville, at that time the capital of
Georgia. Here a small band of Georgia militia tried
to block the way. The Union artillery wheeled into
position and put down a barrage. Veterans of the
Army of the Tennessee, men who had fought at
Shiloh, Vicksburg, Chattanooga and Atlanta, moved
forward, and in moments the fighting was over.

Sherman, coming on the scene, was sickened by what he saw. The Confederate dead were boys of 13 and 14 along with old men, barefooted, some of them clutching weapons that would not have been dangerous at a hundred feet.

From Milledgeville the march went on, leaving behind it a track of almost total devastation sixty miles wide.

And as the army marched on, an army of slaves began to follow. One or two, or ten or twelve, or twenty at a time, they appeared from nowhere to fill the roads between the marching regiments, to overflow the roadsides and spread for miles, a great, flowing river across the winter fields from which the cotton or corn had been gathered a month or two before. They did not know where they were going. They had no idea what lay ahead. They only knew that the men in the blue uniforms represented freedom.

Sitting his horse on a hilltop from which he could see the road winding away in both directions, Sherman watched in amazement. He was primarily a soldier fighting a war. His one purpose was to preserve the Union, with slavery or without it. But neither he nor his soldiers could ever again believe that the Negro did not want freedom.

On December 10, Sherman and his men reached Savannah. There was a small Confederate garrison there and, outside the city, a fort. But the fort was designed to fight off an attack from the sea. From the land Sherman's men easily overran it. Federal ships came up the river bringing new supplies, and the soldiers found it almost a pleasure to eat army rations after the rich diet of the past month.

There was no battle at Savannah. The Confederate garrison, vastly outnumbered, slipped away at night, and the Yankee troops marched into the city.

Savannah was not destroyed as Atlanta had been. There were no important factories here. Many of the people were Union sympathizers. Sherman rested his men and outfitted them with new supplies.

Here he learned that his march to the sea had made his name a byword. Now some congressmen wanted to give him equal rank with Grant. Some even wanted to demote Grant and put Sherman in command of all the Union armies.

It was an idea that would have tempted most military men. It did not tempt Cump Sherman. He had never put personal ambition ahead of what he believed was good for the army, and he did not believe that a promotion at this time would help the war as a whole. Quickly he wrote to his brother John, the senator: "I deem it unwise to make another Lieutenant General, or to create the rank of General. . . . I will accept no commission that will tend to create a rivalry with Grant. I want him to hold what he has earned and got."

With that out of the way, and his men rested, Sherman led his army out of Savannah into South Carolina in January 1865. It was a march that in many ways would make the one through Georgia look like a month-long picnic.

First, the country north of Savannah was naturally swampy, cut by innumerable rivers and creeks. Winter rains had overflowed the streams and flooded the swamps. In Richmond, Jefferson Davis felt certain that Sherman's army could not move northward until spring.

But the Army of the Tennessee was no ordinary army. Years of war had taught these men to fight and take care of themselves; and before the war most of them had been farm boys or frontiersmen from what were then the western states of Iowa, Indiana, Illinois and Ohio.

They could walk all day without growing tired, and they knew how to use axes and mauls and hammers. They cut down trees and built roads through the swamps, and bridges across the streams, and hauled their artillery across. They moved so rapidly that General Johnston, who had finally been recalled to command what was left of Hood's army, told a friend in amazement, "There's been no such army as Sherman's since the days of Julius Caesar."

More terrible than the swamps and winter weather, however, was the attitude of Sherman's army toward the state of South Carolina.

South Carolina had been the first state to secede from the Union. Many people in the North, and even some in the South, blamed South Carolina for the entire war. While Sherman was still in Savannah, General Halleck had written him from Washington: "Should you capture Charleston, I hope that by *some accident* the place may be destroyed, and if a little salt should be sown upon the site, it may prevent the growth of future crops of nullification and secession."

127

Sherman had written back that "The whole army is burning with an insatiable desire to wreak vengeance upon South Carolina. I almost tremble at her fate, but feel that she deserves all that seems in store for her."

Sherman's bark, as General Thomas had said, was often worse than his bite, but this time he was truly expressing the feelings of his men. Now the whole army seemed to feel a personal satisfaction in destroying everything they could lay their hands on. In Georgia many houses had been left undamaged. In South Carolina almost everything bigger than a Negro's cabin was destroyed.

One soldier wrote home: "Our line of march through this state was marked by smoke in the day and the glare of fire at night." Another wrote happily that "The rich were put in the cabins of the Negroes; their cattle and corn were used for rations, their fences for campfires, and their barns and cotton gins for bonfires. It seemed to be decreed that South Carolina, having sown the wind, should reap the whirlwind."

Later, people in the South would say that if a crow had flown across the path of Sherman's army it would have had to carry its own rations, since there wasn't enough left to feed even a bird.

The destruction reached its peak in Columbia, the capital of the state.

Confederate cavalry held the city briefly, but there were only a few of them. As Sherman's army formed a battle line, the cavalry slipped out of town on the far side. The army marched in unopposed, and Sherman, riding his horse down one of the city's streets, found great piles of cotton on fire.

"Who started this fire?" he asked.

"Confederate cavalry," he was told. "Just before they left town."

This was quite possible. Confederate troops often burned their cotton before retreating in order to keep it from being confiscated. Sherman rode on and set up his headquarters in a large empty house. His plan was to quarter the army in the town for several days and let it rest.

He had been there only a few hours when his orderly announced, "A woman to see you, sir. Says she's an old friend of yours."

"Send her in."

The lady who entered was about Sherman's age, and he recognized her immediately. He had known her twenty years before when, as a young lieutenant, he was stationed in Charleston. "I live here in Columbia now," she told him, "and I wanted to thank you for protecting my house. Not even my chickens or ducks have been bothered."

"I'm glad," Sherman said. "Only I don't think you should thank me. I didn't even know you were living here now."

The lady laughed. "I understand that. Some of your soldiers came to my home about an hour ago. I don't know what they might have taken, or done. They were leading my horse out of the stable when I saw them. I told them I was a friend of yours."

"And they believed you?"

"Not at first. But you may remember, twenty years ago in Charleston you gave me a book, and wrote your name on the flyleaf. I still have it. I showed it to the soldiers and they all took turns looking at it, and one of them said, 'That's Uncle Billy's handwriting. I know it.' So they not only put my horse back in the stable; they left a guard outside."

"The guard is there now?"

"Inside the house now," the lady said. "He's taking care of my baby while I came to thank you."

It was Sherman's turn to laugh. "You tell him my orders are to take good care of that baby and to protect your property as long as we are here."

The lady left, and Sherman went back to his work. The cotton bales he had passed while riding into town continued to burn; a wind began to blow.

Nobody knew just how the first houses caught fire. One hundred years later, people would still be arguing this question. Perhaps the wind blew bits of burning cotton onto nearby roofs. Perhaps drunken soldiers set the fires. Certainly many of the soldiers resting in Columbia that night were drunk, and certainly they had been burning houses and towns since they left Atlanta. However it happened, here and there houses began to burn. The sky turned faintly pink with the flames. And the fires spread.

What followed was a kind of fantastic nightmare. The flames leaped higher, leaped from house to house, shot upward in great red and orange banners against the sky. The earth itself seemed a writhing mass of black shadows and flame-colored lights. People were running and screaming. Terror-maddened horses plunged in and out of flaming barns.

At his headquarters Sherman was notified soon after the fires began. He ordered troops to fight the fires, then went himself to make sure it was done. What he found was a wild inferno. Some soldiers battled heroically to put out the fires, and some ran shouting through the streets carrying flaming torches to start more fires. The wind was blowing hard now. The crackling sound of the flames mingled in one unearthly roar with the shouts of men, the screams of women and children, the terrible shrieks of horses trapped in burning stables.

When daylight came, Columbia, South Carolina, was little more than a mass of ashes.

One of the few houses not destroyed was the one in which Sherman had made his headquarters. He immediately moved out, set up his headquarters in a tent and turned the building over to women and children.

What had been the city of Columbia was still smoldering when Sherman and his army marched away into North Carolina. Here the troops did not feel the personal bitterness and anger they had felt in South Carolina, and there was not so much burning and looting. Even so, the army still lived off the land. With no base and no supply train, there was no other way.

There were a few short, sharp battles. General Johnston was still as shrewd and determined as ever. He struck at Sherman's flanks whenever there was a chance, but the blows were light. Johnston simply did not have the strength to offer any real opposition. The Union army moved steadily northward, closer and closer to Richmond.

14

A National Hero

The war was coming to a close.

General Robert E. Lee's Army of Northern Virginia had fought long and gallantly, but now it was worn to a fraction of its former strength and pinned down by General Grant in front of Richmond. Sherman's army was approaching Richmond from the south, and neither Lee nor Johnston had any power to stop it. To anyone who looked clearly at the matter, it was obvious that the South could not resist much longer.

At this point Sherman left his army in North Carolina and took a steamer to visit General Grant. Together the two officers went to call on President Lincoln. "Mr. President," Sherman said, "there will probably have to be one more large, bloody battle. But it should destroy the Southern armies and end the war."

Lincoln groaned. "Can't we end it without any more fighting? There has been so much bloodshed already."

Sherman saw the lines of pain in Lincoln's face and realized the burden the President had borne. But he shook his head. He believed another battle would be necessary, and Grant agreed with him. Finally Lincoln nodded. "If it must be," he said.

Lincoln then went on to tell his two generals what surrender terms they could accept. The war had been fought to preserve the Union and to destroy slavery. Lincoln did not want to destroy the South. He favored generous terms that would allow Southern soldiers to return to their homes, go back to work and begin to rebuild the states that had been devastated by the war.

With the President's instructions clear in his mind, Sherman went back to his troops in North Carolina. He began to lay plans for a last major battle.

Actually there would never be such a battle. By now Grant's army had almost encircled Richmond, and in a desperate attempt to save what was left of his own army, Lee was forced to abandon the city. But now he led only a tattered and starving fragment of an army. Within a few days it was trapped by Grant's forces. And on April 9, 1865, at Appomattox Courthouse, Virginia, Lee surrendered.

Even so, the war was not quite over. The Confederate army, led by Joseph Johnston, still existed. But Johnston sent Sherman a message asking that they meet and talk over the terms of surrender.

Sherman agreed immediately. By this time his army had reached Raleigh, North Carolina, and the two generals made plans to meet at a farmhouse between their forces on the morning of April 17.

Sherman planned to make the first part of the short trip by train. As he climbed aboard, a telegraph operator came running down the track. "General!" he shouted. "There's a coded message coming over the wire for you. Do you want to wait until it's decoded?"

"Where's it from?"

"From Washington, General."

"I'll wait," Sherman said. The message, he thought, might be from President Lincoln with more information about the terms of surrender to be accepted.

The telegraph operator ran back to his office. Thirty minutes later he was at the train again. His face was white now, and his hand shook as he handed the decoded message to Sherman.

It was not from Lincoln. It was from the secretary of war. It was dated two days before and it read: "President Lincoln was murdered about ten o'clock last night in his private box at Ford's Theater in this city, by an assassin who shot him through the head with a pistol ball. . . ."

Sherman's hand began to tremble. He knew the men in his army had worshiped Lincoln. He knew that word of the President's murder might send them on a terrible rampage, destroying Raleigh in their fury. His face set, he turned to the operator. "Have you told anyone what's in this message?"

"No, sir."

"Then don't. Not a soul. Do you understand?"

"Yes, sir."

Sherman folded the telegram and put it in his pocket. He gave a signal, and the train began to move. But all the way to his meeting with Johnston he was remembering his last conversation with President Lincoln and Lincoln's desire to bring the South back into the Union as quickly and easily as possible. This was how Sherman himself felt. Now he was glad to accept Johnston's surrender on much the same generous terms Grant had given Lee.

When he returned to Raleigh, Sherman ordered his troops confined to camp. Only then were they told of Lincoln's murder, and in his message Sherman made it clear that neither the Confederate army nor the people of the South as a whole were responsible.

With Johnston's surrender, the war at long last should have been over. In the sense of armies opposing one another in the field, it was over. But even before Lincoln's death many persons in the federal government had favored punishing the South for its rebellion. Now these people came into power. They insisted on changing the generous surrender terms Sherman had granted. Unless the South was punished, they said, it would soon start another war. Some of the newspapers and politicians who had never liked Sherman claimed that by his surrender terms he was trying to start another war in which he could make himself dictator. Some newspapers actually accused him of treason.

Few persons believed these charges, and they were soon forgotten. Sherman and Grant were the heroes of the hour, and in many ways Sherman's war record was more spectacular than Grant's. Sherman had been the hero of Shiloh. Grant had been the commanding officer at Vicksburg, but in this

William Tecumseh Sherman

same campaign the long, swift marches of Sherman's men had caught the popular imagination. And throughout the final year of the war it was Sherman's accomplishments that had cheered the Union and given men heart to carry on.

In front of Richmond the federal and Confederate armies had battled back and forth over the same bloody ground where they had already fought for three years; but in the west, Sherman's army had gone slashing down through Georgia. The capture of Atlanta had virtually guaranteed the reelection of Lincoln and the final Union victory. The March to the Sea had torn the Confederacy to tatters and put an end to the last Rebel hopes. Yet in all this, Sherman had concentrated on the destruction of property rather than of life: except for the bloody battle of Shiloh, the loss of life in the west, both by Union and Confederate forces, had been far less than in the east.

As national heroes, either Grant or Sherman could have been elected President, but Sherman had absolutely no political ambitions. Instead he was happy to get away from Washington and take command of the army in the far West. His wife Ellen went along. By now his children were grown up. Here in the West he tried to keep peace with the Indians and helped with the building of the first transcontinental railroad.

This was the kind of work that he had always loved. He spent long days riding across the western plains, meeting with Indians in their camps or following the progress of the steel rails as they stretched ever westward. A soldier who rode with

136

him made notes of General Sherman's behavior:

> . . . *he acted like a boy turned loose—threw off reserve—asked 1,000 questions of everybody —never at a loss for a story or joke . . . with a long stride he paced up and down constantly, never weary—a prodigious smoker and talker —stretched in blankets before the fire in the shadow of the mountains, he talked the night half away.*

Many of the railroad workers had served as soldiers under Sherman during the war. Some of them still wore their blue uniforms. Often as Sherman rode past the men would shout to him, "Hello, Uncle Billy. Remember Georgia?"

Sherman would rein in his horse, laughing. "Down there I taught you fellows how to tear up a railroad. I never thought I'd see you out here building one."

To give the men working on the railroad better protection from the Indians, Sherman made many changes in the army organization. But at the same time he tried to make and keep peace with the Indians. He wrote to Grant that some settlers wanted all the Indians killed, but "I will not permit them to be warred against as long as they are not banded together in parties large enough to carry on war."

During one of his meetings with the Indians, Sherman was asked by an old chief for a cannon mounted on the fort wall, an ancient, rusty gun of no real use. "I'll give it to you," Sherman said, "if you promise not to use it to kill soldiers."

The Indian grinned. "Use cannon kill cowboys. Kill soldiers with club."

Happy with his work in the West, Sherman was as determined to keep out of politics as he had ever been. But against his will he was called back to Washington on several occasions. President Andrew Johnson was feuding with members of his cabinet over problems of Southern reconstruction, and knowing that Sherman was sympathetic toward the South, the President wanted to make him secretary of war. This was a political post, and Sherman would have none of it. Washington, he said, was full of "spies and slanderers." He wrote Johnson that he could not bear living in "this political atmosphere," and wound up his letter: "Therefore, with my consent, Washington never."

Still the President wasn't satisfied. He next offered to make Sherman a full general with rank equal to Grant's. Again Sherman refused. It was, he said, a "false position" in which he would have no real duties.

But in 1869, when Ulysses S. Grant became President, Sherman willingly went to Washington to take over Grant's former post of commanding general. He and Grant were old friends and Sherman felt sure they could work together. Indeed, long before, they had planned how to reform army organization and eliminate much of the red tape.

It took him only a few unhappy months, however, to realize that Grant as President was very different from Grant the general. Now he was far more interested in politics than in effective military organization. When Grant suddenly canceled an important order merely to please some politicians, Sherman rushed to see him. "You can't do this," he said. "It's not right."

"Well," Grant said, "if it's my own order, I can change it, can't I?"

For a moment Sherman stared at him, then jumped angrily to his feet. "Yes, Mr. President, you have the power to revoke your own order. You shall be obeyed. Good day, sir." He stalked out.

Later the quarrel between the two men was patched up, but the close personal rapport they had known as soldiers was never to be fully restored.

If Sherman didn't care for many of the politicians surrounding Grant, it was equally true that many of them didn't care for him. Little by little they whittled down his powers as commanding general. Since the country was at peace, this left him little to do. He made a tour of Europe; he wrote his memoirs; he avoided Washington as much as possible.

After Grant went out of office and Rutherford B. Hayes became President, Sherman found his job far more pleasant and less tangled in politics. He became more relaxed and happier, perhaps, than he had ever been, spending much of his time traveling around the country, going to banquets and making speeches.

During one of his speeches, Sherman noticed there were many young people in his audience. Looking at them he said, "There is many a boy here today who looks on war as all glory. But, boys, it is all hell."

A newspaper shortened this to read: "War is

hell." Quickly the saying spread around the world. It became one of the two most famous remarks William Tecumseh Sherman ever made.

He made the second remark four years later, after having retired from the army. Although he still had no interest in politics, an increasing number of individuals asked him to run for President. He kept refusing. To one politician he wrote that he would be "a fool, a madman, an ass" to run for President now that he was 64 years old. Even so, people kept after him. In the summer of 1884, when the Republicans held their convention to nominate a candidate, one of the party leaders wired Sherman: "Your name is the only one we can agree on. You will have to put aside your prejudices and accept the Presidency."

The telegram was delivered to Sherman in his office where he was talking with his son Tom. Sherman read it, snorted and, without taking his cigar out of his mouth, wrote an answer: "I will not accept if nominated, and will not serve if elected."

When the message reached the Republican convention, the politicians could scarcely believe it. No one had ever rejected a Presidential nomination in such blunt terms. But there could be no doubt that Sherman meant what he had said, and soon his words were famous all over the country.

Sherman's refusal to take part in politics seemed to make him more popular than ever. A historian has described the last years of his life as "one big chicken dinner." He was constantly invited to parties all over the country. He left St. Louis and moved to New York because, a friend said, "St. Louis got too slow for him."

When his wife Ellen died in 1888 Sherman went into a kind of retirement. They had been very fond of each other, in spite of some disagreements and long periods of separation. By now most of his children had married and moved away, but two of his daughters still lived with him. But even after Ellen's death he did not remain at home.

On February 4, 1891, Sherman gave a theater party in New York for some old army friends. Afterward he rode home through the snow. Next morning he awoke with a cold. By February 8, his 71st birthday, he was seriously ill. Six days later, on February 14, 1891, William Tecumseh Sherman was dead.

Three men who had been Presidents of the United States attended Sherman's funeral. There were judges, congressmen, governors. There was another man also, at 82 older than any of the others. Bareheaded, his white hair blowing in the raw winter wind, the former Confederate General Joseph E. Johnston stood rigidly at attention.

A young man standing behind Johnston leaned forward and whispered in his ear, "General, please put on your hat. You might catch cold."

Johnston did not move. When the casket had passed and the funeral carriage had moved away, he turned to the young man. "If I were in General Sherman's place, and he were standing here in mine, he wouldn't have put on his hat either."

It was, perhaps, the finest compliment one great old soldier could have paid another.

Chronology

February 8, 1820—Born in Lancaster, Ohio.

June 1829—Goes to live with Thomas Ewing's family after the death of his father.

1836—Enters West Point.

1840—Graduates from West Point and is assigned to duty in Florida.

September 1853—Resigns from the army to take a bank job in California.

October 1859—Becomes superintendent of the Louisiana State Seminary of Learning and Military Academy.

May 14, 1861—Appointed colonel in U. S. army.

July 21, 1861—Battle of Bull Run.

Fall 1861—Called "insane" by some newspapers, and temporarily relieved of his command.

January 1862—Returns to duty with the army.

April 6–7, 1862—Battle of Shiloh.

December 1862–July 1863—Battle of Chattanooga.

May 5–September 2, 1864—Campaign across northwestern Georgia, ending with the capture of Atlanta.

November–December 1864—March to the Sea, from Atlanta to Savannah, Georgia.

January–April 1865—Campaign through South and North Carolina.

April 9, 1865—Lee surrenders to Grant at Appomattox Courthouse.

April 17, 1865—Sherman meets with Confederate General Joseph Johnston to discuss surrender of Johnston's army.

June 5, 1884—Sherman wires the Republican Presidential Convention: "I will not accept if nominated, and will not serve if elected."

February 14, 1891—Dies in New York City.

For Further Reading

Catton, Bruce, *The Centennial History of the Civil War*, Doubleday & Company, 3 volumes, 1965.

Catton, Bruce, *This Hallowed Ground*, Doubleday & Company, 1956.

Hart, Liddell, *Sherman, Soldier, Realist, American*, Frederick A. Praeger, 1958.

Lewis, Lloyd, *Sherman, Fighting Prophet*, Harcourt, Brace and Company, 1932.

Milton, George Fort, *Conflict, The American Civil War*, The Infantry Journal, 1941.

Nichols, R. F., *Battles and Leaders of the Civil War*, 4 volumes, Yoseloff, 1957.

Rhodes, James Ford, *History of the Civil War*, Frederick Unger Publishing Company, 1961.

J6520

921
SHE

Blassingame, Wyatt

William Tecumseh
 Sherman: defender
 of the union

DATE			